Imperial War Museum

First World War Posters

Joseph Darracott and Belinda Loftus

Preface

The Imperial War Museum's poster collection first became the basis of a major public display in the temporary War Posters Exhibition of 1972. This seemed a good opportunity to publish in two booklets a selection of reproductions relating, in one case, to the First World War and, in the other, to the Second. It may be hoped that these will serve either as a permanent reminder of the temporary exhibition or as a source of interest independent of it.

The Museum's collection of posters was formed largely through the initiative of my predecessor, the late Mr L R Bradley, who served the Imperial War Museum in one capacity or another for nearly 50 years. It now amounts to some 50,000 items and it continues to grow through gifts, exchanges and purchases.

The Trustees are very grateful to those who have helped to enrich the collection by presenting posters to it or by offering advice and information about it. On the basis of this and of our own research and observation we have built and are extending a bank of specialised information to which I would particularly draw the attention of students of the subject who may, I believe, find it useful.

The Keeper of the Art Department, Mr J C Darracott, has been primarily responsible for the two booklets as he was for the exhibition but it is fit that I should mention the special contribution of Miss B M Loftus of his Department. I also wish to acknowledge the valuable help of the Head of the Department of Photographs, Mr D P Mayne, the Principal Photographer, Mr F J Dicker, the Keeper of the Department of Education and Publications, Dr C Dowling, who edited the booklets and guided them through HMSO, and Mr A Garrett, who was responsible for their design.

Noble Frankland
Director

Imperial War Museum
1972

For this second edition (1981) minor corrections and a few replacements of images have been made.

Introduction

This booklet about war posters in the Imperial War Museum aims to make better known the range and importance of the Museum's collection. There are more than 30,000 posters and proclamations from the First World War—not only from Britain but also from America, Austria-Hungary, France, Germany and other countries, including the British Empire. The other most important collections of war posters in Europe are in Stuttgart, Koblenz, Vienna and Paris. The Bibliothek für Zeitgeschichte, Stuttgart, contains a good collection of German posters of the First World War. The Bundesarchiv in Koblenz is particularly valuable for German political material. The Musée des Deux Guerres Mondiales, Paris, has a collection of about five thousand posters, mostly French. In addition some libraries and print rooms have war posters in their collections. Preparatory work for this booklet has included consulting the print rooms of the Victoria and Albert Museum, the Bibliothèque Nationale, Paris, and the Albertina, Vienna. The present compilers have not seen the two main American collections at the National Archives (formerly the collection of the Library of Congress) or that of the Hoover Institute of War, Revolution and Peace. There are also collections of war posters in other European museums and libraries, and American universities, including Harvard and Yale.

It has proved difficult to discover how many war posters are held in public collections. At present no international survey of war posters appears practicable, while much material is listed but not catalogued. Curators and librarians will certainly be glad when the nearly universal problems of storage and conservation of posters can be overcome, and their collections made more easily available for study by well-qualified students, whether of art, history, psychology or sociology. A special difficulty in the study of posters is the large number extant. It seems to the present compilers that many general statements about posters and their history, even in works of reference, are ill-founded.

The figures for poster production in the First World War are startling. The war created a need for government publicity on a scale quite beyond that of commercial advertising campaigns. Before the war the British Museum had the right to a copy of every poster printed, but during the war, owing to the extent of poster production, this right was renounced. The Fourth American Liberty Loan, for which ten million posters were produced, was the largest campaign mounted in American history. In every country the story was the same—massive campaigns being used by governments, especially to obtain money for war loans.

The extent of British war poster production was considerable, but its organisation was unusual. The war savings posters were in the first instance less pervasive than recruiting posters, many of which were produced for the Parliamentary Recruiting Committee. The Committee was made up from all political parties, and its aim was to use the party organisations for recruiting; local party helpers not only distributed posters but also delivered circulars to electors to ask them to come forward as recruits when called on by the War Office. The Committee's work was successfully carried out and only ceased when conscription was introduced in 1916. The commissioning of posters, however, was often done in a haphazard way. A suggestion would be made by a printer and approved by the Committee. The poster would then be drawn up and published. 'Daddy, what did you do in the Great War?' is a case in point. Mr Paul Gunn of Johnson, Riddle and Company, told the story in a letter to the Museum: 'One night my father, so the story goes, came home very worried about the War situation and discussed with my mother whether he should volunteer. He happened to come into where I was asleep and quite casually said to my mother, "If I don't join the forces whatever will I say to Paul after the war if he turns round to me and says 'What did you do in the Great War, Daddy?'"' He suddenly turned round to my mother and said that would make a marvellous slogan for a recruiting poster. He shot off to see one of his pet artists, Savile Lumley, had a sketch drawn straight away, based on this theme projected about 5 years hence, although by the time it had taken shape the questioner had become one of my sisters. To end the story on a nice note, he joined the Westminster Volunteers a few days after.'

One result of posters being produced by printers was that many of them have a direct and simple working-class appeal. They contrast with work produced for charities, run by aristocratic or middle-class ladies, who commissioned well-known artists like Louis Raemakers or J P Beadle to draw posters. Incidentally, there were so many British charities that an Act of Parliament was passed in 1916 to enforce their registration, and a National Scheme of Co-ordination of Voluntary Effort was established.

The casual way in which Parliamentary Recruiting posters were commissioned did not reflect a lack of organisation in the advertising industry. On the contrary, *The Placard*, the journal of the United Bill Posting Association, regretted the un-professional conduct of the government's publicity campaigns. The Association, however, had a long history of conflict with Parliament, where more than one attack was made during the war. There was consequently much less co-ordinated effort between the government and the billposting interests than in the United

States, where spectacular hoardings were put up and painted with *Wake Up America* or posters for the navy. Some professional designers turned to government work, for example Frank Brangwyn, who was responsible for a distinguished series of posters. Brangwyn had designed some of his earliest posters for shipping lines, which, together with the railways, were important promoters of poster design. The London Underground is deservedly the best known, for its active policy of commissioning first-class work under the direction of Frank Pick; during the war this tradition was worthily maintained by commissions which included posters to be sent out to troops at the front.

After America's entry into the war in 1917 poster production there was highly organised. The story is told in *How we advertised America* by George Creel, who was in charge of the government's Committee of Public Information. The Committee's work included organising canvassers for recruiting, finding men willing to make brief speeches (the Four Minute Men), and using the services of the Division of Pictorial Publicity, which was the name given to a group of artists whose chairman was Charles Dana Gibson. These artists offered their designs free to government departments and other organisations, and produced a staggering total of 1438 drawings and designs in all. The American publicity campaigns included many sorts of ephemeral material like flag day emblems and button badges, as well as huge hoardings outside public buildings. There were, besides, many posters produced in art colleges, such as the Art Institute of Chicago. The whole subject is relatively well documented and deserves a modern study.

In France, Germany, Austria-Hungary and Italy there was a more general aware-ness of the artistic interest of posters. The German Verein der Plakatfreunde produced a magazine, *Das Plakat*, which exemplified this artistic interest and which differs sharply from the trade magazines of Britain (*The Placard*) or America (*The Poster*). One method of promoting posters was through competitions, which were hardly used at all in Britain or America, but which had been a normal part of commercial advertising on the European continent before the war. It is worth noting, however, that in every country there was an interest in war posters, and many exhibitions were held, such as that of Russian War Posters (Hotel Plaza, New York, 1917), British Recruiting Posters (Berlin 1915), Italian Artists and the War (including poster designs, London 1916). One fact which emerged in preparing this booklet was that many poster designers had studied abroad; this makes it easier to understand why the posters of artists from different countries seem to have close affinities. An example is the lithographic style found in the work of Steinlen, Fouqueray, Brangwyn and Spencer Pryse. Realistic illustrations, as used for magazines, can be found in every country, though they predominated in the United States.

Against the international interest in posters and their connections must be set those posters which have an unmistakably national flavour. The general character of the French posters in our collection is that they are drawn, rather than composed in blocks of colour, and that they carry a relatively long text. This is a little surprising since one of the most successful poster designers of pre-war Paris was the Italian, Leonetto Cappiello, whose reputation was based on brilliant colour and simplified images, with which commercial products became closely identified. Cappiello himself did little poster work during the war, being employed in the Italian Information Service.

Single dominant images are more often found in our German posters. The acknowledged master is Ludwig Hohlwein, whose style owes something to the Beggarstaffs whose work he knew from his stay in England; but there are other designers of similar distinction. German designers seem to have been given a freer hand than designers elsewhere, so that German posters have more abstract images than were used in Britain and carry less text than was normal in France. The typography was also of a higher standard, and was normally designed by the artist, not added by the printer as happened in Britain. After the war Nazi propagandists looked coldly on these First World War posters, condemning them for being ineffective; but in fact we have no way of measuring the effectiveness of posters at that time. Almost all that can be asserted about a poster is that it was popular, or, as in the case of the Kitchener poster, that it was widely imitated.

Sometimes the same posters were used by both sides in the war; this could be plagiarism but in some cases was propaganda. German orders in Belgium were, for example, reprinted in Britain. The editor of one such booklet, called *Scraps of Paper: German proclamations in Belgium and France*, described the posters as 'inhuman documents, which are printed to enable the reader to enter more fully into the feelings of those who, for two long years, had been subject to a reign of terror'. Another instance of posters being used for propaganda is the group of anti-German posters produced to persuade Americans that it was time that their country entered the war. This group includes a poster showing a child with hands cut off, one of the unsubstantiated allegations of atrocities made against Germany. Posters used in this war are one aspect of the psychological warfare which became intense in the First World War. Nevertheless few posters achieved the violence of cartoons, or the ferocity of prints (of which the Museum holds a good collection,

8

mainly French, presented by the fifth Marquess of Bute in 1951). Some posters went too far for public opinion: Frank Brangwyn's poster for a war loan, showing a British soldier bayoneting a German, had the slogan 'Put Strength into the Final Blow'. After protest this was amended, being considered unacceptable for its brutality. This sort of case tells us clearly about the feelings of a period; posters are of value as historical evidence and can help us to form a correct interpretation of other sorts of evidence, where truth may be more readily concealed or falsehood more easily suggested.

A famous false image on a poster was New York in flames, drawn by Joseph Pennell for the Fourth Liberty Loan. The image showed New York destroyed by a bombing raid, at that time an impossibility. The poster has an additional interest because its production was described in detail by the artist from sketch to final printing. The poster was produced by two printers using different methods, and it was issued as a supplement to a magazine. Pennell's booklet can serve as a concise guide to the techniques of poster production in the war. His poster was a lithograph. Lithographs might either be drawn directly on a stone or a plate and printed, like those of Spencer Pryse. They might be done on paper, and transferred to a stone or plate. They might be watercolour or oil paintings, re-drawn or photographed onto a plate. They might be printed directly from the plate, wound round a cylinder, or transferred to a blanket and printed or set off from a cylinder. We have used the term 'autolithograph' in this booklet only where we know that the drawing was done by the artist himself. Pennell did an autolithograph for his Liberty Loan poster. He sent it to a poster competition, the only print among many drawings. His opinion of American printers sank very low when he found that the printers had costed his lithograph for re-drawing on to a stone, not realising that it was already printed.

A modern observer cannot help being intrigued by the psychology of First World War posters. Were hate posters really tolerated? Were atrocity posters believed? Was a poster with a slogan like 'Women of Britain Say Go!' or 'Daddy, What Did You Do In The Great War?' persuasive? It is particularly difficult to know whether the undertones of a poster were recognised at the time. Today a constant barrage of publicity has created a critical awarenesss of the means of persuasion which must then have been largely absent; further, our eyes can translate a more abbreviated visual language and often find war posters over-emphatic.

Finally the aim of this booklet cannot be to give a definitive account of First World War posters. We have stressed in our entries the variety of poster designers' careers; we note that there are different ways in which posters could be examined, discussed or used as evidence. Voltaire's words are our apology: 'The most useful books are those in which half the matter is provided by the readers themselves; they bring to flower those thoughts whose seed is presented to them; they correct what seems to them defective and they strengthen by their reflections what seems to them weak.'

Acknowledgments

We wish to thank the following individuals and institutions for the valuable and knowledgeable help we have received.

Mr S C F Allen (Mills & Allen Ltd); Olave, Lady Baden-Powell; Bibliothèque Nationale, Paris; Dr Bisanz (Museum der Stadt Wien); Mr Rodney Brangwyn; British Museum Library & Mss Department; British Transport Historical Records; Mr Nicholas Brown (Leicester Galleries); Herr Buck (Stuttgart Bibliothek für Zeitgeschichte); Professor P Fehl; Dr Fritz (Heeresgeschichtliches Museum, Vienna); Professor Fritz Grossmann; Mr Paul A Gunn (Johnson, Riddle & Co Ltd); Miss Paula Harper; Miss Joan Hassall; Institut d'Art et d'Archaeologie, Paris; Mr Neil Kinsey (Johnson, Riddle & Co Ltd); Herr Horst Herbert Kossatz (Albertina Vienna); Mlle Claude de Lestang Laisné (Musée des Deux Guerres Mondiales, Paris); Mr H Mallatratt (British Poster Advertising Association); Miss Clelia Matania; Mr Franco Matania; National Széchényi Library, Budapest; Amsrat Sagl (Österreichische Nationalbibliothek, Vienna); Herr Anton Sailer (Müncher Stadtmuseum); Times Library; United States of America Embassies in London and Paris; Victoria and Albert Museum Library and Print Room; Mr B R Watson (John Waddington, Kirksall Ltd); Westminster City Reference Library; Frau Widlar (Albertina Vienna).

We also thank the following members and former members of the Museum's staff for varied but essential help.

Mr M H Brice; Miss R E B Coombs; Mr B L Kitts; Mr J Lucas; Mr M D Moody; Mr B D Slade; Mrs R Sharman; Mrs J Mosley; Mr P J Simkins; Mr J O Simmonds.

Responsibility for any inaccuracy remains that of the compilers, who will be glad to have note of additions or corrections.

Select Bibliography

There is no thorough modern study of First World War posters. We have a file of bibliographical references, to which qualified students can have access, but most of the material listed is general and not specifically about war posters. Almost none is held by the Imperial War Museum.

General Surveys
Hardie, Martin and Sabin, Arthur K. *War Posters issued by belligerent and neutral nations 1914–1919*. London, 1920
Rickards, Maurice. *Posters of the First World War*. London, 1969.
Darracott, Joseph. *The First World War in Posters*. New York, 1974

Austria
Massiczek, Albert and Sagl, Hermann. *Zeit an der Wand*. Vienna, 1967. (A well-illustrated survey of posters illustrating the history of Austria in the twentieth century. Both world wars are covered. Sound comment on the political background)

France
L'Affiche et les arts de la publicité. Paris, 1928. (A special number of this periodical is about war posters)

Germany
Gehrig, Oscar. *Plakatkunst und Revolution*. Berlin, 1919
Arnold, Friedrich. *Deutsche Plakate als Dakumente der Zeit 1900–1960*. (Covers German posters in the same way that *Zeit an der Wand* does Austrian Posters)
Das Plakat. 1914–1918. (This periodical was published throughout the war for the Verein der Plakatfreunde)
Handbücher der Reklamekunst
I Die Sammlung Angewandter Graphik (private collections)
II Künstler-Zeichen (monograms)
III Schriften über Reklamekunst (bibliography)
IV Unsere Reklame Künstler (short autobiographies and self-portraits of artists)

Great Britain
The Placard. 1914–1916. (This periodical ceased publication in 1916 and was not resumed until after the war)
Sheldon, Cyril. *A History of Poster Advertising*. London, 1937
Haste, Cate. *Keep the home fires burning: propaganda in the First World War*. London, 1977

Italy
Rubetti, G. *Un'Arma per la Vittoria*. Milan, 1917
Rubetti, G. *La Publicità nei prestiti italiani di guerra*. Milan, 1919. (Two volumes published by Il Risorgimento Grafico)

United States of America
The Poster. 1914–1918. (A good account of the American campaigns in this periodical)
Creel, George. *How we advertised America*. New York, 1920. (A short but valuable account of 'the Battle of the Fences')
Pennell, Joseph. *The Liberty Loan poster*. New York, 1919

Exhibition catalogues
Fehl, Philipp and Fenix, Patricia. *World War I Propaganda posters*. University of North Carolina, Chapel Hill, 1969
Harper, Paula. *War, Revolution and Peace*. Stanford University Museum of Art 1971

Theses
Unpublished work on war posters or poster design includes
Lubbers, L E. *L'image publicitaire actuelle et ses origines*. Institut d'Art et d'Archaeologie, Paris
Pauker, P. *Heinrich Lefler*. Vienna
Kitzwegerer, L. *Alfred Roller*. Vienna

Photographic Survey
Wild, Wolfgang. *Das politische plakat*. 9 volumes 1925–1952. (Typescript and hand-coloured photographs. Wide-ranging survey of European political and war posters covering both wars. In the Bundesarchiv, Koblenz)

Lord Baden-Powell

Robert Stephenson Smyth Baden-Powell was born in London on 22 February 1857, the son of the Reverend Professor Baden Powell and Henrietta Grace Smyth. After attending Charterhouse from 1870 to 1876 he entered the army where he enjoyed a distinguished career from 1876 to 1910, serving mainly in India and Africa. He is chiefly renowned for holding Mafeking during the Boer War and for his work for the Boy Scout movement, which he launched in 1908.

Baden-Powell showed artistic talent from an early age. He was an ambidexterous sketcher (a fact which worried his mother till she was reassured by John Ruskin, who showed Baden-Powell his art collection), and later in life he both illustrated his books with his own drawings and watercolours and supplemented his meagre army pay by sending drawings to illustrated journals, notably the *Graphic*. He designed various playbills for the amateur theatricals which he organised during his early career but *Are You in this?* appears to be his only war poster. It was No. 112 in the Parliamentary Recruiting Committee series and when it was deposited at the Imperial War Museum by the PRC and the Stationery Office was described as a 'picture typifying the unity of all classes in the common aim.' It is a typical PRC poster both in style and sentiment.

In 1912 Baden-Powell married Olave St Clair Soames. They had one son and two daughters. In 1929 he was created Baron Baden-Powell and he received many decorations, British and foreign. He died in Kenya on 8 January 1941.

DESIGNED BY LT. GEN. SIR R.S.S. BADEN POWELL.

Are **YOU** in this?

PUBLISHED BY THE PARLIAMENTARY RECRUITING COMMITTEE, LONDON. POSTER NO.112.   PRINTED BY JOHNSON, RIDDLE & CO. LTD., LONDON. S.E.

IWM Cat No: 2712

1915 **Are YOU in this?**
$29\frac{3}{4} \times 19\frac{1}{2}$ ins; 75·5 × 49·5 cms
lithograph
signed RBP

J P Beadle

James Prinsep Beadle was born in Calcutta on 22 September 1863, the son of Major-General James Pattle Beadle RE. When he was thirteen Beadle became a pupil of Joseph Edgar Boehm and then studied under Alphonse Legros at the Slade on a three-year scholarship. He subsequently attended the Ecole des Beaux-Arts in Paris and became a pupil of G F Watts in London. Beadle exhibited at the Royal Academy from 1884 and he also exhibited at the New Gallery and elsewhere. In 1891 he married Anna M G Cope.

Beadle painted landscapes, animals, figures and portraits but his speciality was military subjects. In 1889 he won a bronze medal at the Paris Universal Exhibition for his painting *Her Majesty's Life Guards;* two of his 1914–18 war pictures are in the Museum, *Zero Hour* and *The Breaking of the Hindenburg Line.* He appears to have designed two posters during the First World War. The one illustrated here was poster No. 36 in the series issued by the National War Savings Committee, a body responsible for a large number of First World War posters. His other poster was a plea not to waste food. Both show how an academic English genre-painter, albeit a good one, failed to create a visually effective poster, particularly as compared with contemporary work in Germany. The Germans designed the text as part of the poster, and virtually eliminated all half-tones, reducing the design to a simple formula legible from afar; Beadle and many other English artists like him included detailed drawing and soft half-tones only discernible on close inspection, and left the lettering to the printer.

Beadle died in London on 13 August 1947.

1917 **It's worth While! That's Why**
$29 \times 19\frac{3}{4}$ ins; $73 \cdot 7 \times 50 \cdot 2$ cms
lithograph
signed and dated J P Beadle 1917

W T Benda

Wladyslaw Theodore Benda was born in 1873 in
Posen, Poland. He studied at Cracow Academy
and by the beginning of the 1914–18 war was
established as a mural painter and illustrator in
New York.

Give or We Perish is a typical example of the
romantic feeling in Benda's work. He drew an
equally appealing girl for a Young Men's Christian
Association poster. He also designed three
recruiting posters for Polish patriots in America,
one of which inspired the following verse:
'See the winged Polish warrior that Benda has
                                                                        wrought!
Is he private or captain– I cannot tell which,
For printed below is the patriot thought
Which Poles pronounce 'Sladami Ojcow Naszych.'

Benda was mainly known after the war as a maker
of masks, and he wrote the entry on modern
masks for the Encylopaedia Britannica. Making
masks began as a hobby during the war; after it
some of his masks were illustrated in *Vanity Fair*
and used privately. Benda masks were later used
in theatrical productions and photographed on
Vogue models by Edward Steichen. Some masks
are character studies, like those of Abraham
Lincoln or Paderewski, but those used by dancers
are more generalised, like The Golden Peacock,
Silly Doll and Golden Goddess. The story is
charmingly told by the artist himself in *Masks*,
published in New York in 1944. Benda died in
New York in 1948.

GIVE OR WE PERISH

AMERICAN COMMITTEE
FOR RELIEF IN THE NEAR EAST
ARMENIA ~ GREECE ~ SYRIA ~ PERSIA
CAMPAIGN *for* $30,000,000

IWM Cat No: 2754

Give or we perish
$31\frac{5}{16} \times 21\frac{1}{4}$ ins; $79 \cdot 5 \times 54 \cdot 0$ cms
photo-gravure
signed W T Benda

F Boehle

Fritz Friedrich Boehle was born in Emmendigen.i.B. on 7 February 1873. He was a pupil of Hasselhorst at the Städel in Frankfurt and then studied with W Diez at Munich Academy until 1892. He was a painter, a graphic artist and a sculptor. From 1894 until 1896 he worked in Munich; he then moved to Frankfurt.

Boehle's work was strongly influenced by the old masters, Dürer, Cranach, Schongauer, Mantegna and Donatello. This particular war loan poster draws heavily on a woodcut by Dürer, reinforcing its request for money with an appeal to Germany's medieval religious traditions. (For other variations on the medieval knight-in-armour theme see pages 35 and 39).

Boehle's work is in many German museums and there have been various exhibitions devoted to him, notably a memorial exhibition at the Frankfurt Kunstverein in 1916–17. He died at Frankfurt on 20 October 1916.

Thanks be to God.
Givst thou a mite
Be it ne'er so small
Thou shalt be blessed by God

1915 **In Deo Gratia**
$28\frac{5}{16} \times 22\frac{7}{8}$ ins; $71 \cdot 9 \times 58 \cdot 1$ cms
lithograph
signed and dated F Boehle 1915

Frank Brangwyn

Frank Brangwyn was born in Bruges on 13 May 1867, the son of William Curtis Brangwyn, an English architect and interior decorator. Brangwyn returned to London when he was eight; he subsequently attended South Kensington School of Art and spent three years with William Morris before travelling in Europe and the East. He was a prolific artist in many media and also designed craftwork. He married Lucy Ray who predeceased him; they had no children.

During the 1914–18 war Brangwyn produced much visual propaganda, including a large number of posters and poster stamps, mostly for recruiting and for charities, particularly Belgian charities. Several of his designs were given free. The poster illustrated here was printed by the Avenue Press, who are said to have printed all his war posters. A proof of it, bearing Brangwyn's scribbled instructions to the printers, is in the Victoria and Albert Museum. There is also a horizontal version with the slogan *Back him up— Buy War Bonds* (see page 61). Brangwyn's war posters are a superb example of the artist-lithographer's approach. They were given an appreciative article in the German poster magazine *Das Plakat* but Brangwyn is said to have been criticised in Britain for portraying the seamy side of war. There is certainly a vicious element in this example, but some of his charity posters are deeply moving and he later became a pacifist.

Brangwyn exhibited widely in Britain and Europe and there have been various memorial exhibitions since his death. An artist of international reputation, he is represented in many museums, notably the Brangwyn museums at Bruges and Orange (France), at Swansea and in the William Morris Gallery at Walthamstow. In 1941 he was knighted. He lived at Ditchling, Sussex, where he died on 11 June 1956.

Put strength in the final blow
60 × 39¾ ins; 152·4 × 101·0 cms
auto-lithograph
lettered Auto-Lithograph by Frank
Brangwyn ARA

Bernhard

Lucian Bernhard was born in Vienna on 15 March 1883. He studied at Munich Academy and in Berlin under Growald, who encouraged him to become a poster artist. His successful career was started by his winning design for Priester matches in 1905. He worked in Berlin until he went to New York in the 1920s. Called by Julius Klinger 'the Father of the Poster', Bernhard designed many trade posters which nearly always consist of a strong simple image of the product with its name. Rademacher has aptly described this as 'telegram-style'. Bernhard also created well-known types such as Fraktur, Antiqua and Kursiv; his typographic posters are always superb and instantly recognisable as his work. He also designed interior decorations and was one of the first important German designers of his day to handle ephemera such as book-covers and trade-marks.

During the 1914–18 war Bernhard produced innumerable posters, mainly for war loans and nearly all typographic rather than pictorial. This poster was designed for the Seventh War Loan (see page 66). It was also produced in a smaller version than the one shown here. The mailed fist used in it is a powerful symbol of aggression, which has subsequently been replaced in Communist and Black Power propaganda by the naked clenched fist. It is interesting that Bernhard has matched his 'Gothic' Fraktur type-face with a 'medieval' woodcut technique for the fist. For a similar return to medieval German symbolism and technique see F Boehle's poster (page 16). The appeal to historical nationalism is obvious.

In 1920 Bernhard became the first professor of poster design at the then Royal Academy of Berlin. He settled in the USA in 1923. He has taught in New York and was co-founder of the design firm Contempora.

This is the way to peace— the enemy wills it so! Therefore subscribe to the War Loan!

1917 **Das ist der Weg zum Frieden**
$25\frac{3}{4} \times 18\frac{1}{2}$ ins; $65\cdot4 \times 47\cdot0$ cms
lithograph
lettered BERN
HARD

Biró

Mihály Biró was born in Budapest on 30 November 1886. He studied at the Budapest School of Arts and Crafts and then from 1908 to 1910 in Berlin, Paris and London. In 1910 he won first prize in a poster competition organised by *The Studio*. Between 1910 and 1919 he worked in Budapest as a poster designer, painter, sculptor and graphic artist. He became well known for his posters decrying social evils and agitating for political reform. Perhaps the most famous is his poster for the *Népszava* journal, which shows a worker swinging a large hammer.

During the 1914–18 war Biró designed a number of striking posters. The example illustrated here is one of two very similar posters on the same theme; the other shows a woman running away from a burning house with two children in her arms. The firm, swirling, black outlines and the large areas of brilliant colour used in both of them are typical of Biró's bold, flowing designs. In 1917 there was an exhibition of Biró's work in the Ernst Museum in Budapest.

Biró took an active part in the Hungarian revolutionary movement and was poster commissar during the Hungarian Soviet Republic in 1919. After the overthrow of the republic he emigrated to Vienna and then to Berlin, and finally fled from the Nazis to America. He returned to Hungary in 1947, a very sick man, and died in Budapest on 30 November 1948.

A lottery for artists to help rebuild villages ruined by Russian troops in northern Hungary. Exhibition in the Museum of Fine Arts, Budapest.

Müvész-Sorsjáték
$37\frac{5}{16} \times 24\frac{1}{2}$ ins; $94\cdot7 \times 61\cdot6$ cms
lithograph
signed Biró

IWM Cat No: 0506

19

G Capon and Geo Dorival

Georges Dorival was born on 5 November 1879. He studied at the Ecole des Arts Décoratifs in Paris, and became editor of *L'Art et la Mode*; his work includes many railway posters, and others for shipping lines. G Capon is presumably Georges Louis Capon, a decorative artist who exhibited at the Salon des Tuileries and the Salon des Indépendants. There is one poster by G Capon in the Bibliothèque Nationale, where he is described as a poster artist.

The partnership of Capon and Dorival was responsible for several war posters, another in the Museum being designed for a campaign against tuberculosis, which is symbolised by a snake. The two posters are similar in style and quite different from the fine lithographic drawing of artists like Steinlen.

The German eagle was often used in First World War posters (see also page 30), usually in a naturalistic or heraldic treatment. More abstracted eagle forms can be seen in post-war inflationary currency and in National Socialist propaganda emblems.

Two Scourges:
The German, Tuberculosis
The German eagle will be defeated
Tuberculosis must also be defeated

1917 **2 Fléaux**
　　　　Le Boche
　　　　La Tuberculose
$45\frac{3}{4} \times 31\frac{1}{2}$ ins; 116·2 × 80·0 cms
lithograph
signed Geo Dorival 17 and G Capon

Howard Chandler Christy

Howard Chandler Christy was born in 1873 in Morgan County, Ohio. He studied in New York at the National Academy of Design and under William Chase at the Art Students League. He first made his name during the Spanish-American War, when he went with the United States troops to Cuba and sent back drawings which were used by *Scribners* and *Leslie's Weekly*. The first of the Christy Girls was done at this time for a picture called 'The Soldier's Dream', reproduced in *Scribners*.

This poster, which was produced by photolithography, was drawn and lettered by Christy and is typical of his war poster work. Another of his pretty girls exclaims *Gee! I wish I were a Man! I'd Join the Navy!*

Christy gave more time to painting portraits after the war; his sitters included Mrs Calvin Coolidge, Mrs William Randolph Hearst and Secretary of State Hughes. He also taught at different times at the Cooper Union, the Chase School, New York School of Art and Art Students League. His mural paintings included decorations for the Café des Artistes in New York, but his most celebrated mural is *The Signing of the Constitution* in the rotunda of the Capitol in Washington DC. Christy died in 1952.

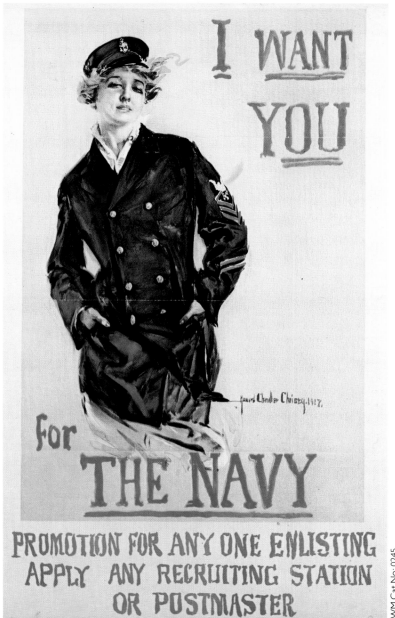

IWM Cat No: 0245

1917 **I Want You for the Navy**
41 × 26¾ ins; 104·2 × 68·0 cms
photo-lithograph
signed and dated Howard Chandler
Christy 1917

G Clausen

George Clausen was born in London on 18 April 1852, the son of a decorative painter. When sixteen he entered his father's firm in order to become a furniture designer. He attended evening classes at South Kensington School of Art and, encouraged by Edwin Long, he won a National Scholarship when twenty to study full-time at the School from 1873 to 1875. Subsequently he worked as Long's assistant and in 1875–1876 visited Belgium, Holland and Paris. Clausen was a painter of rustic scenes, a decorative artist and an engraver. In 1881 he married Agnes Webster; they had three sons and two daughters.

During the 1914–18 war Clausen painted a major oil for the War Artists scheme and contributed several lithographs to the *Britain's Efforts and Ideals* series. This poster is one of a group of four published by the Underground Railways of London at Christmas 1916. At this time restrictions on paper prevented the general distribution of posters at home, but it was possible to send them to the troops overseas to 'awaken thoughts of pleasant homely things'. The drawings were the free gifts of the artists: Clausen, Charles Sims, F Ernest Jackson and J Walter West. Hardie and Sabin stated: 'Everyone who served abroad knows how much these posters were appreciated as a decoration in Army messes, YMCA huts and elsewhere'. The appeal to men's love of England as a country was used again in the 1939–45 war by the *Your Britain—Fight for it Now* series and Walter Spradbery's *Proud City* posters (which, like these, used quotations).

Clausen designed posters for the London, Midland and Scottish Railways during the Twenties under Norman Wilkinson's scheme for posters by eminent Academicians. He exhibited at the Royal Academy and other London societies from about 1875. In 1927 he was knighted. He died on 23 November 1944.

1916 **A Wish**
   $39\frac{7}{8} \times 25$ ins; $101 \cdot 3 \times 63 \cdot 5$ cms
   auto-lithograph
   signed G Clausen

The Underground Railways of London, knowing how many of their passengers are now engaged on important business in France and other parts of the world, send out this reminder of home. Thanks are due to George Clausen R.A. for the drawing.

A WISH. Mine be a cot beside the hill; The swallow oft beneath my thatch Around my ivied porch shall spring The village church among the trees. A bee hive's hum shall soothe my ear; Shall twitter from her clay built nest. Each fragrant flower that drinks the dew Where first our marriage vows were given. A willowy brook that turns a mill. Oft shall the pilgrim lift the latch. And Lucy at her wheel shall sing With merry peals shall swell the breeze With many a fall shall linger near. And share my meal a welcome guest. In russet gown and apron blue. And point with taper spire to Heaven

IWM Cat No: 0340

J U Engelhard

Julius Ussy Engelhard was born at Bindjey in Sumatra on 18 August 1883. He studied at Munich Academy where he was a pupil of Franz von Stuck. He was a painter, a poster designer and an illustrator working for many fashion magazines and for *Simplicissimus*.

Engelhard's posters were influenced by the work of Hohlwein, the leading poster designer in Munich at this time. The example shown here was also produced in another version bearing the text *Bolschewismus bringt Krieg, Arbeitslosigkeit und Hungersnot* (Bolshevism brings War, Unemployment and Hunger). Both posters were directed against the German Spartacus League, led by Rosa Luxemburg and Karl Liebknecht, which attempted to bring about a Communist revolution in Germany in 1918 and 1919. Their accusations must be seen against a background of appalling want. The swift growth of Germany's population in the second half of the nineteenth century made for a dependence on imported foodstuffs. She was therefore particularly vulnerable to the Allied blockade during the First World War. Deaths from actual starvation and from diseases caused or aggravated by malnutrition rose dramatically. It is true that the armistice in 1918 brought an easing of the blockade but the hunger remained for a long time and reached a new height during the revolutionary period; the Spartacists therefore provided a convenient scapegoat for reactionary groups such as the Freikorps.

It is interesting that the ape-figures so common in Allied propaganda of the 1914–18 war hardly appear in German war propaganda; it is only during the post-war revolutionary period that they are constantly used as a symbol of Anarchy and Bolshevism.

Engelhard died in Munich on 13 December 1964.

Distress and Ruin follow Anarchy

1918 **Anarchie**
$48\frac{3}{8} \times 36\frac{3}{16}$ *ins; 122·9 × 91·9 cms*
lithograph
signed and dated J U Engelhard 18

23

H R Erdt

Hans Rudi Erdt was born in Benediktbeuren on 31 March 1883. He learnt lithography and then became a pupil of M Dasio at the Munich School of Arts and Crafts. From 1908 he was one of the foremost designers of posters in Berlin. He did much work for the printers Hollerbaum and Schmidt.

The large areas of flat colour in the poster illustrated here and the monumental scale are typical of Erdt's work. It is possible that this poster advertises a film or a book. The U motif obviously appealed to Erdt, for he also used it in a poster advertising a wartime film about the Ukraine.

It was apparent to the Germans, particularly after the Battle of Jutland in 1916, that their High Seas Fleet could not break the British blockade. Only counter-blockade could do that. U-boats were ideal for this task, their numbers increasing from 28 in 1914 to a total of 371, of which 178 were lost by the end of the war. At first their use was restricted from fear of international repercussions, but from February 1917 the U-boat war was unrestricted and was a major reason for America's entry into the war.

Erdt died in 1918.

The U-boats are out!

IWM Cat No: 0515

U Boote heraus!
54½ × 36½ ins; 138·4 × 92·7 cms
lithograph
signed H R Erdt

Erler

Fritz Erler was born at Frankenstein on 15 December 1868; his brother was Erich Erler, also an artist. Erler was a pupil of Albert Brauer at Breslau, and then studied at the Academie Julian in Paris before travelling in Italy and North Germany. He was a painter and graphic artist; he also designed mosaics and ceramics and executed many murals in public buildings in Germany. His work has a monumental decorative style, often using German folk-tales or other allegories. He lived in Munich from 1895 to 1918. He was co-founder of the magazine *Jugend* and he was a founder-member of the *Die Scholle* group.

Erler did not serve during the 1914–18 war but did many drawings and paintings of soldiers at the front, some of which were published. In January 1917 he described for the *Suddeutschen Monatshefte* how in October 1914 he had accompanied the Freisinger Jägern and had seen war in all its horror in the area round Lille. He spoke as one haunted by the soldiers he had met: 'You pale apparitions, whitish like new fresco-paintings, in the chalk-hollows and corridors . . . you are always with me, you follow me until your real face becomes plain and you finally take shape as the man with the steel helmet before Verdun.'

This might almost be a description of the poster shown here, which was issued on 23 March 1917 as part of the campaign for the Sixth War Loan. The steel helmet the soldier wears was issued in 1916. This poster was produced in at least three different sizes; it was also produced as a post-card (see page 61).

From 1918 Erler lived at Utting am Ammersee. He died in Munich on 11 July 1940.

Help us Conquer! Subscribe to the War Loan

1917 **Helft uns siegen!**
$22\frac{1}{4} \times 16\frac{5}{16}$ ins; 56·5 × 41·5 cms
lithograph
signed Erler

Abel Faivre

Jules Abel Faivre was born in Lyons on 30 March 1867. He studied under J B Poucet at the Ecole des Beaux Arts, Lyons; he then worked in Paris under Henry Bataille in the studio of Benjamin Constant, and under J Lefèbre. Faivre travelled in Turkey and Palestine, returning to Paris to become a well-known cartoonist for magazines like *Le Rire, Le Journal,* and *Echo de Paris.* His caricatures of doctors were published in a successful album.

Faivre contributed posters to all the campaigns for French war loans. *On les aura!* was done for the Second War Loan but was reissued. The phrase was coined by General Pétain during the Battle of Verdun. The pose of the soldier recalls a sculptured group by François Rudé on the Arc de Triomphe (see page 62), of which a variant figure is the same sculptor's statue of Marshal Ney. Faivre's original drawing is in the Musée des Deux Guerres Mondiales, Paris. The artist had difficulty in finding a soldier to pose for him. He looked for suitable models among the troops arriving at the Gare de l'Est, but the first man who posed was nervous about what people might say. Faivre asked him what his usual job was. He said he was a waiter, so Faivre gave him a tip and sent him away. The second model was more successful.

Faivre's poster was much copied; there was an Italian version in 1918 and in the Second World War an American version was used with the text *We have only just started to fight,* a variant of the famous words of John Paul Jones, the American naval officer, in 1779.

Faivre died in Paris in August 1945.

We will get them!

1916 **On les aura!**
44½ × 31 ins; 113·1 × 78·8 cms
auto-lithograph
signed Abel Faivre 1916

On les aura!

2ᴱ EMPRUNT
DE
LA DÉFENSE NATIONALE
Souscrivez

DEVAMBEZ IMP PARIS

IWM Cat No: 0544

James Montgomery Flagg

James Montgomery Flagg was born at Pelham Manor, Westchester County, New York on 18 June 1877. He was a prodigious draughtsman and began contributing to *St Nicholas* magazine when he was twelve; two years later he was drawing for *Judge* and *Life*. Flagg studied under Twatchman and Carroll Beckwith at the Art Students League in New York. He went to England for a year to work in the Herkomer School, and then spent two years in Paris studying under V Marec, improving his water-colour technique and painting portraits, one of which was hung in the Salon. Flagg returned to the United States to become a well known and successful illustrator.

I want you for U.S. Army is the best known American poster of all time. It has been estimated that more than five million copies and reproductions have been printed. The artist dressed as Uncle Sam and drew himself in the mirror; the pose is taken from the Kitchener poster based on a drawing by Alfred Leete. Flagg was responsible for 46 war posters, and also wrote and directed a film to raise funds for the Red Cross. Flagg's illustrative style changed little over the years and Uncle Sam was used again in the Second World War. An example is a poster to boost production for the war against Japan after the German surrender; Uncle Sam holds a spanner menacingly and the text reads *Jap . . . . You're NEXT! We'll Finish the Job!* Flagg's original Uncle Sam poster has been often parodied and adapted, for example in a poster against the Vietnam war, where the head was replaced by a skull (see page 64).

Flagg was the author and illustrator of several books, including *Celebrities* (1951), a series of caricatures and portraits with comments by the artist. He died in 1960.

1917 **I want you for U.S. Army**
    $39\frac{1}{2} \times 27\frac{3}{4}$ ins; $100 \cdot 4 \times 70 \cdot 5$ cms
    photo-lithograph
    signed James Montgomery Flagg

IWM Cat No: 2747

A E Foringer

Alonzo Earl Foringer was born on 1 February 1878 at Kaylor, Armstrong County, Pennsylvania. He studied in Pittsburgh under H S Stevenson and in New York under Blasfield and Mowbery. He was a mural painter and illustrator.

The Greatest Mother in the World was outstandingly successful. Its appeal lies in a double association linked by the poster to the Red Cross appeal. The first association, with the Virgin and Child, is created by the cradled pose and reduced scale of the figure of the soldier. Secondly, the image of a wounded soldier is reminiscent of Mary with the dead body of Christ. The image was widely used and reappeared in the Second World War; the Museum has a British example printed in London for Lady Gowrie's Red Cross Appeal.

Foringer, besides being an illustrator, designed bank notes for European and Canadian banks. He was responsible for several large mural commissions, including the Baptistry and organ walls at the Church of the Saviour Philadelphia, and murals for the House of Representatives in Utah State Capitol.

1918 **The Greatest Mother in the World**
22 × 14 ins; 55·9 × 35·6 cms
lithograph
lettered A E Foringer

D Charles Fouqueray

Dominique Charles Fouqueray was born at le Maris (Sarthe) on 23 April in a year given variously as 1869, 1871 and 1872. He studied at the Ecole des Beaux Arts under Cabanel and Cormion, winning the Rosa Bonheur prize in 1909. Fouqueray had a distinguished career as a mural painter and was a prolific illustrator for magazines like *Illustration* and *The Graphic* as well as for books.

Fouqueray was responsible for a fine group of war posters, including a Serbia Day poster, an African Troops Day poster, and a poster for war orphans, besides the Cardinal Mercier poster. They show a mastery of lithographic drawing and rich colour. Fouqueray's academic training makes it possible that the composition deliberately echoes the Virgin of Pity, who shields figures with her cloak in medieval and Renaissance painting and sculpture.

The poster was drawn in 1916. Cardinal Mercier was a spokesman for the Belgian people in his requests for food, his opposition to the deportation of Belgian workmen, and his condemnation of the Germans' burning of the Louvain Library (rebuilt after the war partly with funds raised by the Cardinal's tour of the United States at the invitation of President Wilson).

Fouqueray's work is represented in most important French museums. During the war he drew naval scenes and at the front, and he completed a diorama of the re-taking of the fort at Douaumont (29 October 1916) in 1923. Several of his murals are in public buildings. Fouqueray died in 1956.

Cardinal Mercier protects Belgium

1916 **Le Cardinal Mercier protège la Belgique**
$47\frac{3}{16} \times 29\frac{1}{2}$ ins; 119·8 × 74·9 cms
auto-lithograph
signed and dated D Charles Fouqueray 1916

Gipkens

Julius Gipkens was born in Hanover on 16 February 1883. He worked in Berlin as a painter and a poster designer. As a designer he was self-taught although he learnt much from the work of Bernhard. His first designs were for the Hohenzollern-Kunstgewerbehaus, a typical Berlin business, and he also did much work for the printers Hollerbaum und Schmidt, who produced the poster shown here. Although his practice was very large, Gipkens undertook the smallest job with great conscientiousness, designing everything from furniture and shop displays to invitation cards and prospectuses. His posters, whether for commercial products of war purposes, normally tell a story, sometimes using bizarre motifs. His style often has a rococo elegance quite different from the heavy symmetry of Bernhard or Hohlwein.

Gipkens designed a large number of war posters, many of them on the theme of conservation. The poster shown here is one of the finest he produced. The symbolism of the German eagle perching on the battered RAF roundel is immensely powerful. The poster was produced in two different sizes for this exhibition in Berlin and as a small hanging placard for a later exhibition in Munich in 1918.

German captured aircraft exhibition at (Berlin) 20 March 1917 under the patronage of HRH Prince Henry of Prussia

1917 **Deutsche Luftkriegsbeute Ausstellung**
$27\frac{3}{8} \times 18\frac{3}{16}$ ins; 69·5 × 46·2 cms
lithograph
signed Gipkens

IWM Cat No: 0508

Erich Gruner

Erich Gruner was born in Leipzig on 14 November 1881; his brother was Walter Gruner, also an artist. Gruner studied graphic art and book design at Leipzig Academy from 1900 until 1905; from 1905 until 1906 he studied in Paris under J Laurens and at the Ecole des Beaux Arts. In 1909 he spent six months in Spain and he visited France again in 1911. Gruner was a painter, a graphic artist, a book-designer and illustrator, and a designer of posters, stamps, book plates and other printed ephemera.

Gruner served in the German army from 1914 to 1916; he was twice wounded. He published a *War Diary* of twelve linocuts in 1915 and a series of fifteen etchings called *War*. Gruner organised numerous exhibitions in German towns and abroad, notably in Copenhagen in 1918. Most of his war posters are for exhibitions. None of them is dated before late 1916 and it seems reasonable to assume that he only started designing war posters after he left the army. The poster shown here was also produced in a woodcut version. Both versions show clearly the expressionist vein that ran through all Gruner's poster designs. Clearly the subject matter was stimulating, for not only did it encourage Gruner to produce this rather beautiful poster with its interesting use of the symbols of crown and clasped hands, but it also evoked a most striking design from an artist called Wurthmann.

Gruner made two visits to Italy in 1919 and 1920. From 1930 until 1946 he was director of the Leipzig School of Arts and Crafts.

Thanks-offering from the Kaiser and the Nation to the Army and Navy to provide them with Christmas gifts. 1917

1917 **Kaiser- und Volksdank**
$47\frac{1}{4} \times 35\frac{3}{8}$ ins; $120 \cdot 0 \times 89 \cdot 9$ cms
lithograph
signed Erich Gruner

Hansi

Jean Jacques Waltz (known as Hansi) was born on 23 February 1873 at Colmar, Haut-Rhin. His father was the town librarian and became curator of the Colmar Museum. Hansi was an intransigent French patriot, who was glad to escape from German territory to study at the Ecole des Beaux Arts, Lyons. On his return he began to write and illustrate articles and books ridiculing the German authorities in Alsace and Lorraine. His first success was with a series of articles written in German for *L'Express* (Mulhouse) under the name of Professor Knatschke. Like his friend and compatriot, Zislin, his satire brought him before the courts, and *Mon Village* led to his condemnation for high treason at Leipzig in 1914. In July he jumped bail and fled to Switzerland. He joined the French army as a private but was transferred to propaganda work, about which he published an account, *A Travers les Lignes Ennemis*, in 1922 with E Tonnelat.

Hansi's style blends caricature with popular images rather in the style of Epinal. *Images d'Epinal* were coloured woodcuts widespread in nineteenth-century France, treating contemporary subjects. Hansi's portrait of Alsace under French rule is of a fairytale land. He wrote and illustrated eight books on the history and heraldry of Alsace (see page 68).

Hansi succeeded his father as curator of the Colmar Museum in 1923. His successful career was interrupted by the war. In April 1941 he was attacked in the street by two men believed to be from the Gestapo, and left for dead. He again fled to Switzerland, returning to Colmar in 1945, where he died in 1951.

. . . this heaven is our blue sky, this field is our land. This Lorraine and this Alsace are ours!

... Ce ciel est notre azur
Ce champ est notre terre!
Cette Lorraine et cette Alsace, c'est à Nous!
Victor Hugo.

. . . Ce ciel est notre azur
$30\frac{3}{4} \times 23\frac{3}{16}$ ins; $78 \cdot 1 \times 58 \cdot 9$ cms
lithograph
signed Hansi

Hassall

John Hassall was born in Deal in 1868, the son of Christopher Hassall RN. After trying unsuccessfully for Sandhurst and farming in Manitoba with his brother, he decided to make art his career and in the early nineties attended Antwerp Academy and the Academie Julian in Paris. Hassall exhibited large paintings at the Royal Academy and elsewhere, worked as a black and white artist (chiefly for the *Sketch* from 1893 to 1912) and designed many decorative friezes and panels. But he found his true vocation as a poster designer, working on contract to the printers, David Allen, for seven years. He designed theatre and trade posters, using a broad, brightly-coloured, humorous style, typified in his famous *Skegness is so Bracing*. A book on Hassall was published by Blackie in about 1910. He was twice married, to Isobel Dingwell by whom he had one son and two daughters, and to Constance Brooke-Webb, by whom he had one son and one daughter.

This poster, given to the Museum in 1917 by the Belgian Canal Boat Fund, was probably one of the many designs Hassall did free. It stands out from his other war posters by reason of its delicacy. The Fund brought food, clothing and medical aid to civilians behind the Allied lines in Belgium and sent comforts to Belgian soldiers. It was intended to distribute supplies via the Belgian canals but this proved impossible.

The last poster Hassall designed was *Save Poland*, during the 1939–45 war. He was granted a civil pension by King George VI for his services to posters. He illustrated many children's books and published two 1914–18 propaganda books, *Keep Smiling* and *Ye Berlyn Tapestrie*. He died on 8 March 1948.

Belgian Canal Boat Fund
29½ × 19$\frac{9}{16}$ ins; 75·0 × 49·7 cms
lithograph
signed Hassall

Ludwig Hohlwein

Ludwig Hohlwein was born in Wiesbaden on 26 April 1874. After visiting Paris and London he settled in Munich, remaining there until 1944, when he moved to Berchtesgaden. He first studied as an architect but then produced a remarkable series of animal paintings before commencing in 1906 his career as a poster designer, which won him international fame. He also designed printed ephemera, such as prospectuses, packaging and invitation cards. He was married with two daughters.

Hohlwein's early posters were mainly for restaurants, shops and cafés in Munich. They show an awareness of the flat patterning used by the Beggarstaffs in England, together with that superb sense of layout and visual balance which was Hohlwein's main strength. The Beggarstaff influence persists in this poster, but Hohlwein may have worked from a photograph, as he did increasingly later in his career. The impact of this famous poster is reflected in a speech made to the German National Assembly in 1919 by Herr Scheidemann, denouncing the terms of the Versailles Treaty 'All over Berlin we see posters which are intended to arouse a practical love for our brothers in captivity; sad hopeless faces behind prison bars. That is the proper frontispiece for the so-called Peace Treaty; that is the true portrait of Germany's future; sixty millions behind barbed wire and prison bars; sixty millions at hard labour, for whom the enemy will make their own land a prison camp.'

After the 1914–18 war Hohlwein designed travel and political posters, finishing his career by designing posters for the Nazis during the 1939–45 war. He made increasing use of photographs and the airbrush, and his work in this period is marked by a heavy brutality, the seeds of which are in his earlier designs. He died in Berchtesgaden on 15 September 1949.

People's Charity for German Prisoners of War and Civil Internees

Volksspende
$16\frac{3}{16} \times 11\frac{13}{16}$ ins; $41 \cdot 1 \times 30 \cdot 0$ cms
lithograph
signed Ludwig Hohlwein München

34

IWM Cat No: 2746

A Karpellus

Adolf Karpellus was born at Neu-Sandec in Galicia on 8 January 1869, the son of an Austrian major. He studied at the Vienna Academy under Christian Griepenkerl and J M Trenkwald and at the Academie Julian in Paris under Fleury and Lefevre. He was a painter in oil and tempera of portraits, landscapes and still lifes (particularly flowers); he was also a poster designer. He was a member of the Siebener-Clubs and the Vienna Künstlergenossenschaft (1905). A retrospective exhibition of his posters was held at the Wiener Künstlerhaus in 1905.

During the 1914–18 war Karpellus designed war posters and postcards and was one of the selectors for the art section of the 1917 Vienna War Exhibition. The poster illustrated here is one of his finest designs and is representative of the superbly heraldic decorative feeling to be found in Austrian art at this time, whether influenced by Art Nouveau or not. The design makes familiar use of the medieval knight in armour (see pages 16 and 39) and also of the dove, symbolising the peace that will be obtained through a victory facilitated by war loans. To cover the cost of the 1914–18 war the Austro-Hungarian monarchy had to produce the equivalent of two and a half years' revenue in addition to normal expenses, that is, 90 billion Kronen. Eight war loans raised almost 54 billion Kronen between 1914 and 1918. Inflation after the war practically robbed the war loan subscriber of his rights.

Karpellus died in Vienna on 18 December 1919.

Subscribe to the Seventh War Loan

1917 **Zeichnet 7 Kriegsanleihe**
$48\frac{3}{4} \times 36\frac{1}{2}$ ins; 123·8 × 92·7 cms
lithograph
signed A Karpellus

Julius Klinger

Julius Klinger was born in Vienna on 22 May 1876. After three years' study at the Vienna Technologischen Gewerbemuseum (Museum of Technology and Industry) he worked as an illustrator for a number of magazines (mostly humorous) in Vienna, Munich and Berlin. In Berlin in 1897 he started designing posters, which were mostly printed by Hollerbaum and Schmidt. Their success was immediate. These early designs show the influences of Art Nouveau and the work of the Beggarstaff Brothers in England. These influences Klinger later rejected, purifying and refining his work to a series of flat decorative forms executed in a limited number of colours with precisely handled lettering, though still with a taste for the grotesque rather similar to Gipkens. He aimed to make the poster into a symbol, not just a picture with words, remarking that the American flag would be the best poster for the USA because it was the best symbol for that land. Klinger was also a painter and a designer of type-faces, such as Klinger-Antiqua and Klinger-Kursiv. He travelled extensively in France, Britain, Scandinavia and Switzerland.

In 1915 Klinger returned to Vienna, where he worked for the Austrian war archives until 1918 and designed several fine war posters, including this one, which was presumably based on Willy Menz's Sixth German War Loan design (see page 71).

In 1918 Klinger opened his own poster studio in Vienna, where he continued to design trade posters in an increasingly Expressionist style. He exhibited in Berlin and Vienna and produced various books, including *12 Klinger-Plakate* (12 Klinger Posters) published in Vienna in 1923.

Eighth War Loan

1918 **8 Kriegsanliehe**
$37\frac{1}{4} \times 24\frac{3}{4}$ ins; 94.7×63.0 cms
lithograph
signed Julius Klinger

Alfred Leete

Alfred Leete was born in Thorpe Achurch, Northampton on 28 August 1882, the son of a farmer, J A Leete. He was a humorous illustrator who also designed a handful of posters for the Underground Electric Railways and created the trademark for a brewery. He married Edith Webb; they had one son.

During the 1914–18 war Leete designed several posters and contributed a number of war cartoons to magazines such as *The Passing Show* and books such as *All the Rumours* and *The Worries of Wilhelm*, both published in 1916. But his chief claim to fame was his design for the poster shown here. He first designed this image for the cover of the weekly journal *London Opinion*. It was then decided by the Parliamentary Recruiting Committee to use it as a poster. Leete later presented to the Imperial War Museum the design bearing the slogan *Your Country Needs You* (see page 63). This formed the basis of the poster shown here, which was issued in September 1914 (facsimiles can be obtained from the Museum). Note the change in the text, which now ends with *God save the King* (Kitchener insisted that army advertising should always sign off with these words). The poster proved so successful that it was repeated in many different versions (see page 64) and inspired many imitations, including J M Flagg's 'I want you for US Army'. It is still the best-known war poster and has been pirated for many uses. It has recently appeared in the window of a small estate agent's firm in Lambeth as an advertisement for houses; it has also been used as a recruiting poster for the British-American Chamber of Commerce in New York and on a T-shirt.

Leete died in London in June 1933.

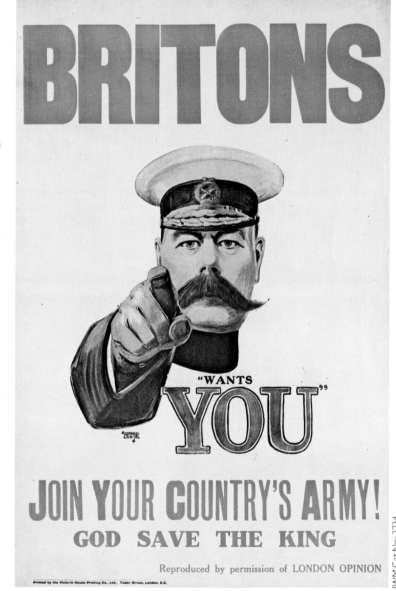

1914 **Britons**——'wants You'
$29\frac{1}{2} \times 19\frac{7}{8}$ ins; 74.9×50.5 cms
photo-lithograph and letterpress
signed Alfred Leete

Heinrich Lefler

Heinrich Lefler was born in Vienna on 7
November 1863, the son of Franz Lefler, an artist
whose strong interest in the theatre influenced
his son. He studied under Christian Griepenkerl
at the Vienna Academy in 1884 and under
Wilhelm Dietz and Nicolaus Gysis at Munich
Academy. Lefler was one of the chief masters of
decorative painting in the Secession style. He
designed interior decorations, furniture, stage-
sets, posters and illustrations. In 1900 he and Josef
Urban founded the Hagenbund the second most
important modern art society in Vienna after the
Secession. Lefler was its president from 1900 until
1903. He was artistic adviser to the Hoftheater
from 1900, and from 1903 until 1910 he was a
professor at the Vienna Academy. Lefler also
acted as artistic director of the Winternitz
clothing firm, was head of Blaschke and Komp,
another clothing firm, and ran an interior
decoration and stage design firm with Joseph
Urban. In 1908 Urban and Lefler collaborated on
the festivities for the sixtieth anniversary of Franz
Joseph's accession.

The poster shown here was one of Lefler's last
commissions. The design reflects the heraldic
geometric style which succeeded Art Nouveau in
Viennese art and design. The two-headed eagle is
one of Austria's national symbols.

Subscribe to the Fourth War Loan

1917 **Zeichnet 4 Kriegsanleihe**
$46\frac{1}{2} \times 34\frac{1}{2}$ ins; 118·2 × 87·7 cms
lithograph
signed HL

M Lenz

Maximilian Lenz was born in Vienna on 4 October 1860. He studied at the Vienna School of Applied Art and was a pupil of Wurzinger and Eisenmenger at the Vienna Academy. He held a Rome scholarship for two years. He was a painter in tempera, oils and watercolour, a sculptor and a lithographer. He was a member of the Vienna Secession from 1898; several of his pictures, including one of the Secession being used as a military hospital in 1916, were shown in the Vienna Secession exhibition at the Royal Academy in 1971.

During the 1914–18 war Lenz designed several elegant war loan posters. The image of St George and the Dragon used in the poster shown here was a convenient symbol for the good nation destroying the wicked enemy, and frequently recurs in posters issued by both sides during the war. There is a British recruiting poster issued by the Parliamentary Recruiting Committee which is very similar to Lenz's design. If plagiarism took place it must have been a case of Lenz copying the British poster, which can only have been issued before the introduction of conscription in 1916; certainly Lenz's version is far superior, showing a peculiarly Austrian feeling for heraldic design.

Lenz died in Vienna on 18 May 1948.

Subscribe to the Sixth War Loan

1917 **Zeichnet die Sechste Kriegsanleihe**
$27\frac{3}{4} \times 20$ ins; $70 \cdot 5 \times 50 \cdot 8$ cms
lithograph
signed M Lenz

J C Leyendecker

Joseph Christian Leyendecker was born in 1874 at Montabour, Germany; he lived in the United States from 1883. Leyendecker studied at the Art Institute of Chicago and at the Academie Julian in Paris under J P Laurens and B Constant. He returned to the United States to practise as an illustrator.

Leyendecker worked for the Division of Pictorial Publicity. This poster was produced by the United States Fuel Administration, which was one of the many organisations to which the Division of Pictorial Publicity proposed designs. Leyendecker and his brother Frank X Leyendecker also worked for the Navy. The Navy had been the first government department to have posters; Lieutenant Commander Henry Reuterdahl had been appointed to act as the Navy's artistic advisor in 1917, before the country had entered the war.

J C Leyendecker did more than three hundred covers for the *Saturday Evening Post* between 1900 and 1940, and was the originator of the Arrow Collar Man, a well-known American publicity campaign. Leyendecker died in 1951.

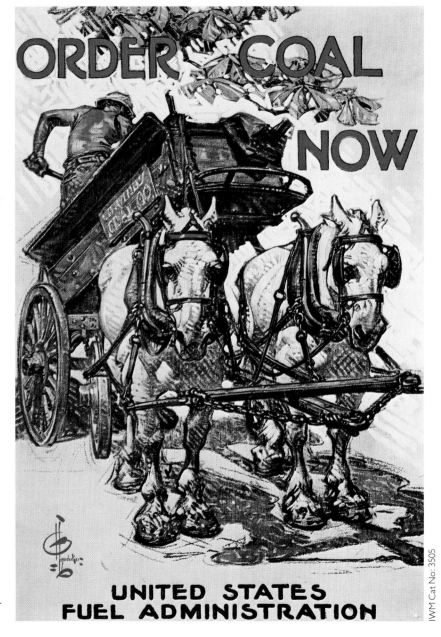

Order Coal Now
29⅝ × 20⅛ ins; 75·2 × 51·0 cms
lithograph
signed J C Leyendecker

Norman Lindsay

Norman Alfred William Lindsay was born in Creswick, Victoria, Australia on 23 February 1879, the son of Dr Lindsay. At the age of sixteen he was engaged to draw illustrations for a Melbourne sporting paper. In 1901 he joined the *Sydney Bulletin* and was its chief cartoonist for many years. He visited England in 1911. He was twice married and had two sons, Jack Lindsay and the late Philip Lindsay, both writers.

The poster illustrated here was one of six Lindsay designed for the last recruiting campaign carried out by the Government of Australia during the 1914–18 war; he also designed the illustrations to three leaflets used in this campaign, which was a highly organised operation (see page 65). The posters were produced in three sizes: 10 inches deep for use on the windows of trains, trams and ferry-steamers; 20 inches (as here) for shop windows and hotels; 40 inches for wherever space permitted. On a prearranged night '?', which had been widely and secretly distributed, was pasted up on every available site. It was a great surprise to the public and caused much discussion. When interest and curiosity were at their height the second poster *Be Quick* was exhibited and was followed by the others – *God Bless Daddy*, *Will you Fight?*, *The Last Call* and *Fall In* – at intervals of seven to ten days. Simultaneously an appropriate mailing notice was sent to each eligible man. Before the last two posters were issued the armistice was signed and the campaign abandoned. The savagery of these designs is arresting. Lindsay believed that 'A country that kills the killer in man will be destroyed by any other country which has preserved the instinct to kill.' (Preface to *Norman Lindsay's Selected Pen Drawings*, 1968).

Lindsay illustrated many books with the fantastic products of his imagination and achieved world-wide success with his etchings, watercolours and oils. In 1957 he published *My Mask*, which tells the story of his life up to 1920. He died on 21 November 1969.

1918 **?**
    20 × 15 ins; 50·8 × 38·2 cms
    lithograph

IWM Cat No: 3242

F Matania

Fortunino Matania was born in Naples on 16 April 1881, the son of Professor Eduardo Matania (1847–1929) and the cousin of Ugo Matania, both of whom were artists. Matania trained in his father's studio and subsequently went to Milan as a special artist for the *Illustrazione Italiana*. At the age of twenty he was working for the *Illustration Française* in Paris and for *The Graphic* in London. After a period of military service in Italy he returned to London to work for *The Sphere*. While employed by them he travelled widely, attending the Delhi Durbar in 1911. Matania married Elvira di Gennaro; they had one son and one daughter. His first wife died in 1952 and in 1960 he married Ellen Jane Goldsack.

Matania produced several hundred war pictures, his drawings of the Russo-Japanese war being famous. He tended to reconstruct events rather than report them, although during the 1914–18 war, when he was acting as war correspondent for *The Sphere*, he visited the front several times. The Imperial War Museum has one oil and one watercolour by him from this period. The poster illustrated here started life as a drawing in *The Sphere*. It is a true illustrator's work of the period, full of near-Victorian sentiment and executed with extraordinary finish and detail.

After the war Matania's illustrations continued to appear in many magazines in this country, in Europe and America. In 1931 he became a writer of historical stories. During the thirties he designed posters for railway companies and holiday resorts. He exhibited at the Royal Academy from 1918, in major London exhibitions and in Italy. Many of his paintings are in regimental collections. He was awarded the Durbar medal in 1911 and was made a Chevalier of the Crown of Italy in 1918. He died in London in February 1963.

'Help the horse to save the soldier'
$30 \times 20\frac{5}{16}$ ins; $76 \cdot 2 \times 51 \cdot 7$ cms
lithograph

IWM Cat No: 2750

42

Mauzan

The few Italian posters in the Museum's collection are matched by groups of posters from other European countries, such as Bulgaria, and some countries outside Europe, such as Brazil. This First World War material was collected from a wide range of sources – dealers, private collectors and by exchange and gift from poster designers and other museum collections.

There are several posters by Mauzan in the collection; this one is based on the Kitchener poster. It is not the only Italian plagiarisation, since the Faivre poster, *On Les Aura*, was also adapted for a war loan. Another Mauzan poster shows an Alpine soldier with an axe attacking a giant hand stretching over a river marked Piave. Mauzan's posters are in the mainstream of Italian commercial art. They contrast with the flat colour area technique used by German designers or the single striking images of Mauzan's fellow countryman Cappiello, who had achieved an outstanding reputation in Paris. Valuable books by Rubetti document the different sorts of material designed for the Italian war loans, including postcards.

Do your whole duty!
Subscriptions to the Loan accepted at the Credito Italiano

'Fate tutti il vostro dovere!'
$13\frac{1}{4} \times 9\frac{1}{4}$ ins; $33 \cdot 7 \times 23 \cdot 6$ cms
photo-lithograph
signed Mauzan

Nevinson

Christopher Richard Wynne Nevinson was born in Hampstead on 13 August 1871, the son of the author and war correspondent H W Nevinson. He trained under the architectural draughtsman John Fulleylove, and then studied painting at St John's Wood in 1907, and at the Slade from 1912 to 1913, before attending the Academie Julian and the *Cercle Russe* in Paris. He was closely associated with the Futurists. He served in France with the Red Cross and the Royal Army Medical Corps from 1914 to 1916, when he was invalided out. He became an official war artist in 1917, and achieved a success with his war pictures which he was never to repeat. He married in 1915.

This poster, one of the few designed by Nevinson, was to advertise an exhibition in March 1918. It reflects a Vorticist obsession with guns, short harsh words and thrusting angular shapes, together with Nevinson's own fondness for silhouettes against the sky, often a feature in his war pictures. The poster was copied for propaganda use and on 21 July 1918 Nevinson wrote to C F G Masterman at the Museum: 'Could you advise me as to whom to apply on the War Bond Poster Dept as I want to *give* them my red bayonet poster. They seem to want it as I notice they are always cribbing it – and none too well – in some effect or other.'

Nevinson made two visits to America, in 1919 and 1920. During the 1939–45 war he was again employed as an official war artist. He exhibited at the Royal Academy and elsewhere and had many one-man exhibitions in London and abroad. He was the author of the autobiographical *Paint and Prejudice*, published in 1937. He died in London on 7 October 1946. A memorial exhibition was held at the Leicester Galleries in 1947 (see also page 69).

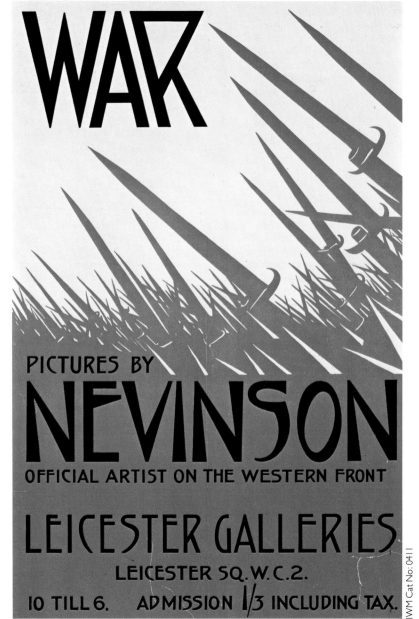

1918 **War**
29½ × 19¼ ins; 74·9 × 48·9 cms
lithograph

Louis Oppenheim

Louis Oppenheim was born at Coburg on 4 May 1879. At the age of twenty he went to London to study, and worked there as a caricaturist and advertising artist from 1899 until his return to Germany in 1906. While in London he first realised the possibilities of lettering in design and his posters for long showed the influence of the Beggarstaff Brothers, with their fondness for flat areas of colour arranged in massive designs. From 1908 he became well known for his work in Berlin.

Oppenheim's 1914–18 designs included many statistical posters with little diagrams comparing the production of vital goods in Germany and Great Britain. These are often signed with the monogram LO. This poster, which was also produced in a version $55\frac{3}{4} \times 37\frac{1}{2}$ ins (141·6 × 95·3 cms) was part of German propaganda's continual campaign to build up Hindenburg as a far greater figure than he was in reality. It was for the Seventh War Loan and is one of Oppenheim's most impressive designs. He was immensely proud of it, claiming that it had been displayed on every street corner and was responsible for Hindenburg's popularity. It certainly compares well with other Hindenburg posters designed by Bruno Paul and Hans Rudi Erdt, although all make a strong impact; clearly the Field Marshal's massive head was a gift to designers. Oppenheim also used Hindenburg in ephemeral material for the Seventh War Loan.

Oppenheim gave further support to Hindenburg by designing a poster for him in the 1932 elections.

The man who subscribes to the War Loan is giving me the best birthday present.von Hindenburg

---

1917 **von Hindenburg**
      $27\frac{1}{16} \times 18\frac{7}{16}$ ins; 68·8 × 46·8 cms
      lithograph
      lettered LOUIS
            OPPEN
            HEIM

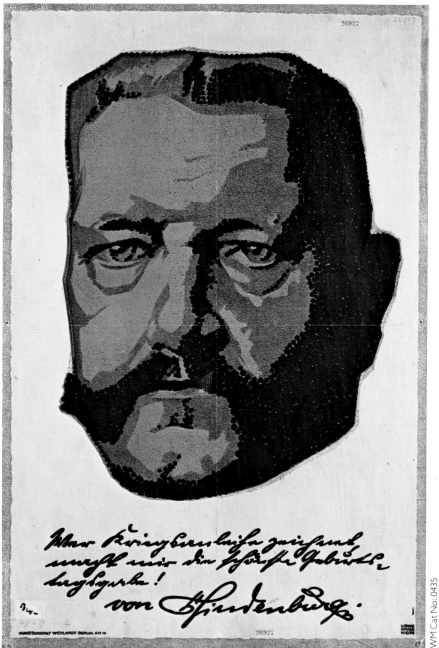

Bernard Partridge

J Bernard Partridge was born in London on 11 October 1861, the younger son of Professor Richard Partridge FRS, President of the Royal College of Surgeons and Professor of Anatomy to the Royal Academy. He was a nephew of John Partridge, portrait painter extraordinary to Queen Victoria. From 1880 to 1884 Partridge designed stained-glass and executed decorative paintings. Later he drew illustrations for books and for the press, joining the staff of *Punch* in 1891. He was one of their most prolific draughtsmen.

The poster shown here is reproduced from Partridge's *Punch* cartoon of 10 March 1915 and was presented to the Museum by the editor of *Punch*. The background to the cartoon was the Clyde Engineers' strike of February 1915, the underlying cause of which was the workers' feeling that large profits were being made by ship-owners while their wages remained unchanged, despite considerable increases in the price of basic necessities such as food and coal. The strike was finally settled on 22 March when wage increases were granted. However, despite propaganda such as this poster, strikes continued throughout 1915. The practice of reproducing cartoons and press illustrations on posters took firm root in the 1914–18 war (see page 42) and was even further developed during the 1939–45 war with the use of work by Fougasse, Giles and H M Bateman. The main difference was that the cartoons of 1914–18 were highly serious whereas their successors in the 1939–45 war were comic. Partridge designed a number of posters during the 1914–18 war, including the much plagiarised *Take up the Sword of Justice* (see page 71) which he produced for the Parliamentary Recruiting Committee.

Partridge was knighted in 1925. He lived in London where he died on 9 August 1945.

"PUNCH," MARCH 10, 1915.

SOLDIERS ALL.

"Tommy" *(home from the Front, to disaffected Workman).*
"WHAT'LD YOU THINK O' ME, MATE, IF I STRUCK FOR EXTRA PAY IN THE MIDDLE OF AN ACTION? WELL, THAT'S WHAT *YOU*'VE BEEN DOING."

IWM Cat No: 2764

1915 **Soldiers All**
30×20 ins; $76 \cdot 2 \times 50 \cdot 8$ cms
letterpress
signed B. P.

Joseph Pennell

Joseph Pennell was born, as recently discovered documents prove, in Philadelphia in 1857. He studied there at the Academy of Fine Arts and the School of Industrial Art. Pennell was an outstanding black and white artist, with a special interest in architecture and topography. He was a friend of Whistler and, with Mrs Pennell, published his biography in 1910. He wrote extensively about graphic arts, notably *Lithography and Lithographers, Etchers and Etching,* and *Pen Drawing and Pen Draughtsmen.*

Pennell thought of recording the war in France, but was unnerved by his experiences at the front. He drew a series of lithographs of industrial work in England and America. After 1917 he was associated with the production of posters for the Division of Pictorial Publicity, of which he agreed to become one of the Associate Chairmen. *That Liberty shall not Perish from the Earth* was a poster for the Fourth Liberty Loan; the imaginary scene of New York in flames from an air raid was a telling image to bring home the idea of war to Americans. Pennell wrote a short book about the poster, published in 1919.

He describes the different printing methods used, including a rather unsuccessful gravure for a magazine of which the Museum also has a copy. The title of the poster was not Pennell's, who favoured a simpler slogan. Pennell died in New York on 23 April 1926

That Liberty shall not perish
$40\frac{1}{2} \times 29\frac{1}{2}$ ins; $102 \cdot 9 \times 74 \cdot 9$ cms
lithograph
lettered Ioseph Pennell Del.

IWM Cat No: 0240

Poulbot

Francisque Poulbot was born at St Denis (Seine) in 1879. Poulbot established himself as a humorous artist who specialised in cartoons of charming and irreverent children. Before the First World War he drew for *Le Rire* and *Sourire* and had published two books of cartoons, *Des Gosses et Des Bonhommes* (Kids and Blokes) and *Encore des gosses et Des Bonhommes*.

The story which this poster advertised was written by Paul Gsell. Poulbot also did a poster for a dramatic presentation called *Verdun* by Gsell, which is in the Museum. The delicate drawing is quite typical of Poulbot's work; he used the theme of children in war for several posters. His other war work included a Soldiers' Day poster (1915) and a War Wounded poster (1917).

Poulbot was a constant book illustrator, and also painted some cabaret murals. He died in 1946.

The Kids in the Ruins

Les Gosses dans les Ruines
44 × 31¼ ins; 111·8 × 79·4 cms
auto-lithograph
signed Poulbot

Louis Raemaekers

Louis Raemaekers was born at Roermond in Holland on 6 April 1869, the son of Josephus Raemaekers and Margaretha Michaelis. He studied in Amsterdam, at Brussels Academy and in Paris. At first he painted landscapes, but from 1909 he worked for *De Telegraaf* in Amsterdam as a political cartoonist. He married Johanna van Mansvelt in 1902; they had three children.

Raemaekers is best known for his anti-German cartoons during the 1914–18 war when he was a strong supporter of Belgium; many of them were published in book form. These cartoons, which, as Raemaekers himself admitted, drew heavily on Forain and Steinlen, expressed intensely bitter feelings with 'a nervous forceful line' (Margaret Whinney's description). They won such renown that in 1916 Raemaekers moved to England so that he could more easily supply the Allied press with them. It was probably shortly afterwards that he designed this poster for the National Committee for Relief in Belgium, an organisation founded in 1915 which used every vehicle of propaganda—postcards, leaflets, newspaper articles and public meetings—to raise money for those still in Belgium. Their first annual report stated that the Executive had distributed 185,000 posters, and in a paper read to the Royal Society of Arts on 24 January 1917 their Honorary Secretary, W A M Goode, said that their propaganda had included 'such striking indictments of Germany as Raemaekers' famous poster depicting the Belgian woman with a terror-stricken child at her breast'. The design was also used as the cover of at least two of the committee's leaflets.

Raemaekers' work was exhibited in Amsterdam and New York. During the 1939–45 war he again designed anti-German cartoons. He died at Scheveningen near The Hague on 26 July 1956.

1916 **In Belgium**
$38\frac{1}{2} \times 23\frac{1}{2}$ ins; $97 \cdot 8 \times 59 \cdot 7$ cms
photo-lithograph
signed Louis Raemaekers

IN BELGIUM

HELP

THE NATIONAL COMMITTEE FOR RELIEF IN BELGIUM,
TRAFALGAR BUILDINGS, TRAFALGAR SQUARE, LONDON.

IWM Cat No: 2711

Alfred Roller

Alfred Roller was born in Brunn on 2 October 1864, the son of Josef and Charlotte Roller. He studied at Vienna Academy from 1883 until 1893, making study trips to Germany, England, France and Holland but chiefly to the Dolomites. He was a pioneering stage designer, painter, graphic artist and poster designer. He was a founder-member of the Vienna Secession in 1897 and its President in 1902; he left with the Klimt group in 1905. From 1900 Roller was a professor at the Vienna School of Applied Art, becoming its director from 1909 until 1935. For two years he ran the magazine *Ver Sacrum*. Between 1903 and 1909 he was head of scenery design at the Vienna Staat Opera. In 1906 he married Mileva Antonie Stoisavljevic.

The poster by Roller shown here is a complete departure from the spare geometric exhibition posters he had designed for the Secession. Nevertheless it is clearly signed with his monogram and although the Madonna is purely Polish the landscape below is the kind of brooding scene Roller often used in his stage designs.

In 1918 Roller returned to his former post as head of scenery design at the Staat Opera, where he remained until 1935. He also designed sets for the Vienna Burgtheater, the Salzburg Festival and productions abroad. In 1934, at Hitler's wish, he designed the scenery for *Parsifal* at Bayreuth. He died in Vienna on 21 June 1935. A memorial exhibition was held in the Landesmuseum at Troppau in 1939.

Honour the graves of the fallen heroes: Lottery to honour the graves of the fallen in Poland. Under the protection of HE Stanislav Skeptychievo: 1 Ticket 4 Kroner. Main prize 100,000 Kr. If drawn in 1920 worth 200,000 Kr. To be drawn 4 June 1918 in Lublin

1917 **Loterya**
$36\frac{1}{16} \times 23\frac{5}{16}$ ins; 91·7 × 59·3 cms
lithograph
signed and dated AR 17

Tito Saubidet

Tito Saubidet Gache (known as Saubidet) was
born in 1891. He studied architecture in Paris at
the School of Architecture from 1910 to 1913, and
painting under Francisco Paolo Parisi. He won a
first prize for posters at the Salon des Humoristes
in 1914, but his profession was architecture.

This poster for an exhibition of paintings is one of
many such in the Museum. Most are posters for
exhibitions of drawings at the front or at sea, but
there are also posters for individual artists and
posters for war memorial exhibitions. Saubidet's
tubular figures recall the simplified shapes used in
cubist painting, although it is clear that his
intention is entertainment, not significant form.

Saubidet was professor of architecture and
perspective in Paris from 1917 to 1928. His
buildings include the Argentinian Pavilion in the
Cité Universitaire, Paris.

Tito Saubidet exhibition

Exposition Tito Saubidet
31 × 23 ins; 78·7 × 58·4 cms
lithograph
signed Tito Saubidet

Lina v Schauroth

Lina von Schauroth was born at Frankfurt a.M. on 9 December 1875. She was a pupil of W Trubner and Ludwig Hohlwein. She worked in Frankfurt as a painter, graphic artist and designer of stained glass and mosaics. During the 1914–18 war Lina von Schauroth designed a number of posters for charities notably a fine series for Christmas gifts to the troops. These posters are nearly always in soft rich tones of grey, brown and purple, using rounded heavy forms of lettering to good effect.

The poster shown here with its rather flatter shapes was a new departure. It appeals for recruits for the Freikorps or Volunteer Corps. These were formed in the winter of 1918–19, in the first place to protect the Eastern frontier of Germany from the Poles and Russians and in the second place to combat the revolutionary Spartacists, in both cases under the slogan of anti-Bolshevism.

In 1960 a one-man exhibition celebrating Lina von Schauroth's 85th birthday was held in the art club at Limpurg House in Frankfurt.

The Hulsen Volunteer Corps 3rd Brigade of the State Army—Reporting Office: Friedberg Hessen-Schloss

Freikorps Hülsen
$34\frac{3}{4} \times 23\frac{5}{16}$ ins; 88·1 × 59·3 cms
lithograph
signed Lina v. Schauroth

Fred Spear

This poster was published in June 1915 by the Boston Committee of Public Safety, after the sinking of the *Lusitania* by a German U-boat attack. More than a thousand civilians were lost, 128 of them American. Spear's poster recalls the drowning of an American mother and child. Without the particular occasion and the word 'Enlist', the dreamlike image of two figures under the sea would arouse no strong response.

The *Lusitania* sinking was widely used for propaganda by both sides. A German medallion was struck commemorating the event, correctly claiming that the ship had carried munitions. The British produced a counterfeit of the medallion, which was widely circulated. The British public interpreted the sinking as a premeditated attack on women and children. The destruction of the *Lusitania* was also a considerable shock to the American public and was a factor in America's decision to enter the war.

1915 **Enlist**
$32\frac{1}{2} \times 22\frac{3}{4}$ ins; $82 \cdot 6 \times 57 \cdot 8$ cms
photo-gravure
signed Fred Spear

Gerald Spencer Pryse

Gerald Spencer Pryse was born in London in 1881. He studied art in London and Paris and was a watercolourist, a lithographer and a poster designer. He married at the age of fifty.

During and after the 1914–18 war Spencer Pryse enjoyed a distinguished service career, attaining the rank of major and winning the Military Cross and the Croix de Guerre. He witnessed the invasion of Belgium and acted as a dispatch-rider for the Belgian Government, visiting all parts of the front line. He based a series of lithographs, *The Autumn Campaign, 1914*, on these experiences. Many of them were drawn on the spot, for Spencer Pryse was a firm believer in the importance of the lithographic stone; even under fire his drawings were made not on paper but on actual stones, carried for that purpose in his car. The poster shown here was produced at about the same time as the *Autumn Campaign* series, and was published by the Underground Electric Railways, by then under the management of Frank Pick, a fine poster patron. Other posters produced under Pick's direction at this time were Brangwyn's *Vow of Vengeance* and a series of four posters sent to soldiers overseas (for an example see page 22). Spencer Pryse designed many other war posters and a well-known series of Labour Party election posters between 1910 and 1929, in which he showed strong compassion for the poor and afflicted. His lithographic technique was superb, exploiting to the full the texture of the stone, the rich sweeping effects of the medium and the expressive qualities of colour.

Spencer Pryse exhibited widely in Britain and abroad. He illustrated many books and from 1907 to 1908 was co-editor of the magazine *The Neolith*. In later life he lived in Morocco. He died on 28 November 1956.

Through Darkness to Light **THE ONLY ROAD** *Through Fighting to Triumph* **FOR AN ENGLISHMAN**

IWM Cat No: 0349

The Only Road for an Englishman
40 × 25 ins; 101·7 × 63·5 cms
auto-lithograph

Steinlen

Théophile Alexandre Steinlen was born in Lausanne on 10 November 1859. He studied in Paris, where he began designing book covers, music covers and posters. Some of these, in a realist vein, had a success comparable to the decorative posters of Jules Chéret or Willette. Steinlen exhibited at the Salon des Indépendants from 1893, specialising in genre subjects, scenes of Parisian life, and cats, which he constantly drew and sculpted. He was a prolific book illustrator.

Steinlen's war posters were designed for the relief of distress in different countries, not only in Belgium but also in Serbia and Russia. Another well-known Steinlen poster is *Sur la Terre ennemie les prisonniers russes meurent de faim* (On enemy ground Russian prisoners die of hunger) whose gaunt figures recall the realist posters Steinlen did for publishers. In *En Belgique* the staring faces emerging from the gloom are paralleled in the work of expressionist painters, like the Norwegian Edvard Munch (born in 1863). Steinlen's drawing is in a tradition of draughtsmanship comparable to the direct lithographic drawing of Spencer Pryse or the designs of Brangwyn. The original design is in the Musée de Deux Guerres Mondiales, Paris.

Steinlen died in Paris on 14 December 1923.

In Belgium the Belgians are hungry
Artistic Tombola....

1915 **En Belgique les Belges ont faim**
$49 \times 36\frac{3}{4}$ ins; $124 \cdot 5 \times 93 \cdot 4$ cms
auto-lithograph
signed and dated Steinlen 1915

Suján

Pál Suján was born in Budapest on 5 May 1880. He attended a school of design in Budapest and later became a teacher of drawing in Pozsony (now Bratislava). He was included in many exhibitions in Pozsony and Budapest, showing mainly portraits and figure paintings.

The poster by Suján shown here is the only one by him known to us. It is one of the most moving posters to come out of the 1914–18 war. As a piece of design it shows that Suján was clearly aware of the work of Van Gogh.

National Exhibition for War Relief, Pozsony July–August 1917. Opening 18 July.

1917 **Landes-Kriegsfürsorge-Ausstellung**
$47\frac{1}{2} \times 24\frac{1}{2}$ ins; $120 \cdot 7 \times 62 \cdot 2$ cms
lithograph
signed Suján

J Paul Verrées

Jean Paul Verrées was born at Turnhout, Belgium, in 1889. He studied at Antwerp Academy and at the Institut des Arts Décoratifs in Brussels. He was in the United States of America during the First World War.

This poster is one of two by Verrées in the Imperial War Museum. The Army Air Service, like the Navy, was dependent on recruiting during the war; only the Army itself had a selective enlistment system. The other poster by Verrées is a visual pun. The image is of the Kaiser in a glass bottle; the slogan encourages conserving fruit and prosecuting the war— *Can the Kaiser*. The Museum holds an interesting group of American posters to promote conservation of fruit and vegetables, and a handful of posters about not wasting other resources.

This poster is particularly interesting for the skill with which textures have been reproduced by lithographic drawing. The rich colours and the evocative figure of the airman make it one of the most decorative posters in the collection.

1917 **Join the Air Service**
37 × 25 ins; 94·0 × 63·5 cms
lithograph
signed and dated J Paul Verrées 1917

Vértes

Marcell Vértes, who later changed his surname to
Vertes, was born at Ujpest in Hungary on 10
August 1895. He attended evening classes at the
Academy of Fine Arts at Budapest and was a pupil
of K Ferenczy. He was a graphic artist, working in
lithography etching and drypoint, a painter in
gouache and watercolour, a stage and costume
designer, an illustrator and an advertising artist.

Vértes served in the 1914–18 war, and designed
political posters in the revolutionary period that
followed. A great deal of his skill was acquired in
this clandestine printing work. This poster, which
probably dates from 1919, shows the fluid
handling and gaiety which are also to be seen later
in his paintings and illustrations. He also designed
in 1919 a poster with the English slogan *Austria's
Agony 1919–20*.

Vértes moved to Paris in the 1920s, where he
became a naturalised Frenchman. He made his
name on his arrival with his album of coloured
lithographs called *Drawings*. He continued his
studies at the Academie Julian and worked with
Jean Paul Laurens. He admired Forain, Degas and,
above all, Toulouse-Lautrec. He illustrated many
books and magazines, chiefly with drawings of
young women. Much of his work was published,
mainly by Pellet in Paris. It seems that he moved
to New York in 1929, returning to France to serve
in the army in 1939–40; that he then went back to
New York and after the war worked there and in
Paris. His work was frequently exhibited, notably
in New York at the Gallery of Modern Art in
1943, at the Carstairs Gallery in 1944 and 1956, at
the Kleemann Gallery in 1951 and in Paris at the
Galerie Charpentier in 1951. He died in Paris in
December 1961.

With me or against me

Velem Vagy Ellenem
$49\frac{1}{2} \times 37\frac{1}{4}$ ins; 125·7 × 94·6 cms
auto-lithograph
signed Vértes

58

Jupp Wiertz

Jupp Wiertz was born in Aachen on 5 November 1888. He attended the Kunstgewerbeschule in Berlin and studied afterwards as a pupil of Eugen Klinkenberg and later of Ernst Neumann. From 1914 he worked as a freelance artist in Berlin, designing posters, packaging, letterheads, book-wrappers and invitation cards. He was also a book illustrator.

The poster shown here won Wiertz the second prize in a competition organised by the Verein der Plakatfreunde (Society of Poster Friends). The competition was judged on 9 June 1918 by a jury including Bernhard and Gruner. The first prize was won by Paul Plontke; Wiertz shared the second prize with Karl Sigrist. Eventually Wiertz's design was actually printed and utilised in this campaign which was run by the Red Cross, along with Plonkte's and that of another prize-winner, Louis Wöhner. As Dr Sachs pointed out in his report on the competition in the *Das Plakat* of September/November 1918 the subject was a difficult one to illustrate and not so frivolous as might appear, for hair was urgently needed for the manufacture of such objects as driving belts for machinery. Wiertz's woman with her offering gesture was a good solution to the problem although it must be admitted that young ladies of this type feature in nearly all Wiertz's early posters.

A one-man exhibition of Wiertz's posters was held in the Deutschen Kulturmuseum at Leipzig in 1917. He designed a large number of travel posters during the thirties. He died in Berlin in February 1939 of blood-poisoning which he caught when spraying a poster.

Women and girls! Collect women's hair! Collection centre at each school.

Local committee for collection and aid service.

1918 **Frauen und Mädchen! Sammelt Frauenhaar!**
$30\frac{1}{4} \times 20$ ins; $77 \cdot 0 \times 50 \cdot 8$ cms
photo-lithograph
lettered Gez: Jupp, Wiertz, Berlin

Frauen und Mädchen!
Sammelt Frauenhaar!
Abnahmestelle jede Schule
Ortsausschuß für Sammel- und Helferdienst
Töpfergasse 33

IWM Cat No: 0434

David Wilson

David Wilson was born at Minterburn Manse, Co Tyrone on 4 July 1873, the third son of the Reverend A J Wilson DD. On leaving school he entered the head office of the North Bank, Belfast, but spent his evenings drawing at the local art school, where his gift for caricature began to develop. The urge to become an artist was so strong that he eventually left the bank and went to London. There, after some difficult years, he became recognised in Fleet Street as one of its leading black and white illustrators. He also painted delicate watercolours of flowers and landscapes.

During the 1914–18 war Wilson contributed a number of war cartoons to *The Passing Show* and published *A verbal and pictorial satire Wilhelm the Ruthless* in 1918. The poster illustrated here was produced in January 1918 by the British Empire Union, an organisation founded in the first year of the war to 'Destroy German Influence, Prohibit German Labour and Boycott German Goods'. The design was first used as a cartoon in the December 1917 issue of the BEU's *Monthly Record*. It was then printed as a poster, which went into many versions, including one printed in Portuguese by the South China Morning Post in Hong Kong; it also appeared as the cover of various BEU leaflets and as a cinema film 'drawn in detail before the audience.' It is a typical example of the many 'hate' posters produced by the British during the war.

Wilson exhibited regularly at the Royal Academy and at the Paris Salon. He died in 1935. Memorial exhibitions of his watercolours were held at the Fine Arts Society in 1935, at Brighton Public Art Galleries in 1937 and at the City of Belfast Museum and Art Gallery in 1938.

1918 **Once a German—Always a German!**
   $29\frac{5}{8} \times 19\frac{13}{16}$ ins; 75·3 × 50·4 cms
   lithograph
   signed David Wilson + W.F.B.

Using a design

It should be realised that many of the posters illustrated in this booklet were produced in a large range of sizes (this is particularly true of German posters). Details have been given of this where possible. Poster designs were used for many other kinds of visual propaganda. Erler's *Helft uns Siegen* was used on a field postcard (1); Raemaekers' *In Belgium* appeared as a pamphlet cover as did Wilson's *Once a German—Always a German!*; and Bernard Partridge's *Take up the Sword of Justice* was produced as a poster stamp (2). In addition some artists produced variants on their own designs. Erich Gruner produced a small wood-cut version (designed to be used as a hanging placard) of his *Kaiser- und Volksdank*. Brangwyn produced two versions of his war loan poster (3 and 4).

IWM Cat No: 2759

IWM Cat No: 0281

Heroes and History

In the propaganda war waged by posters from 1914 to 1918 all nations appealed to their glorious past and to their contemporary heroes to strengthen the resolve of their people. In Britain Alfred Leete's Kitchener poster is the supreme example, but appeals were also made to heroes of a previous era, such as Lord Roberts or 'Bobs', who won the VC during the Indian Mutiny and who was famous for his achievements in Afghanistan and in the South African War (1); and Nelson whose 'England Expects' message was obviously suited to a recruiting poster (2). In France many posters made use of the *Marianne* figure, here seen drawn by Sem, on a poster, from the relief by Rudé on the Arc de Triomphe (3); perhaps the finest adaptation was Abel Faivre's *On les Aura* (4).

1805 "ENGLAND EXPECTS" 1915

ARE **YOU** DOING **YOUR** DUTY TO-DAY?

He did his duty. Will **YOU** do **YOURS**?

on les aura!

2ᴱ EMPRUNT DE LA DÉFENSE NATIONALE Souscrivez

IWM Cat No: 2748

Lord Kitchener

Alfred Leete's Lord Kitchener design started life as the cover of the 5 September 1914 number of the weekly magazine *London Opinion* (1). Leete later presented to the museum the design bearing the slogan *Your Country Needs You* (2). This formed the basis of the Parliamentary Recruiting Committee poster issued in September 1914 (3)—facsimiles are obtainable from the Imperial War Museum. Note the change in the text, which now ends *God Save the King*. Kitchener insisted army advertising should always sign off with these words. Many subsequent versions were issued (4) and Kitchener even appeared on a button-badge (5).

"YOUR COUNTRY NEEDS **YOU**"

IWM Cat No: 2735

DON'T IMAGINE YOU ARE NOT WANTED

EVERY MAN between 19 and 38 years of age is WANTED! Ex-Soldiers up to 45 years of age

"YOUR COUNTRY NEEDS **YOU**"

MEN CAN ENLIST IN THE NEW ARMY FOR THE DURATION OF THE WAR

RATE OF PAY: Lowest Scale 7s. per week with Food, Clothing &c., in addition

1. Separation Allowance for Wives and Children of Married Men when separated from their Families
For a Wife without Children ... 12s. 6d. per week
For a Wife with One Child ... 15s. 0d. per week
For a Wife with Two Children ... 17s. 6d. per week
For a Wife with Three Children ... 20s. 0d. per week
For a Wife with Four Children ... 22s. 0d. per week

2. Separation Allowance for Dependants of Unmarried Men.
Provided the soldier does his share, the Government will assist liberally in keeping up, within the limits of Separation Allowance for, Families, any regular contribution made before enlistment to unmarried Soldiers or Widowers to other dependants such as mothers, fathers, sisters, etc.

YOUR COUNTRY IS STILL CALLING. FIGHTING MEN! FALL IN!!

Full Particulars can be obtained at any Recruiting Office or Post Office.

IWM Cat No: 0414

LONDON OPINION
ONE PENNY.
5th SEPTEMBER, 1914.

Vol. XLII. No. 546.
(Reg. G.P.O.)

This paper insures you for £1000. For conditions see page 374.

"YOUR COUNTRY NEEDS **YOU**"

50 Photographs of YOU for a Shilling.

See Page 400.

BRITONS

"WANTS **YOU**"

JOIN YOUR COUNTRY'S ARMY!
GOD SAVE THE KING

Reproduced by permission of LONDON OPINION

IWM Cat No: 2734

"DEEDS NOT WORDS" 1916

Kitchener's influence

Leete's Lord Kitchener is the best-known war poster of all time and has inspired countless imitations. In Britain during the 1914–18 war pseudo-Leetes were soon on the hoardings (previous page, 4); it was also copied by the Italian artist Mauzan for a war loan poster (1) and in America James Montgomery Flagg based his *I Want You* poster on it (2), which in its turn has been used as the basis for a contemporary anti-Vietnam War poster produced by Personality Posters (3). In Britain during the 1939–45 war there were numerous adaptations; not surprisingly one of them, designed by Bill Little, used Churchill, who was the figurehead during this war that Kitchener was in 1914–18 (4).

2

I WANT YOU
FOR U.S. ARMY
NEAREST RECRUITING STATION

IWM Cat No: 0255

4

DESERVE VICTORY!

1

"Fate tutti il vostro dovere!.."

LE SOTTOSCRIZIONI AL PRESTITO SI RICEVONO PRESSO IL
CREDITO ITALIANO

IWM Cat No: 3509

3

I WANT YOU
FOR U.S. ARMY
NEAREST RECRUITING STATION

IWM Cat No: 2524

An Australian campaign

1914–18 posters were not always isolated appeals but often part of highly-organised campaigns, such as the Government of Australia's last recruiting campaign, for which Norman Lindsay designed six posters and three leaflets. It was to be a cumulative attack on the consciences of men who had not yet enlisted, with the posters displayed in sequence, '?' (page 41) followed by *Quick!* (1), *God Bless Daddy* (2), *Will you Fight?*, *The Last Call* (3) and *Fall In*. Simultaneously leaflets were to be distributed (4) and an appropriate mailing notice sent to each eligible man. Before the last two posters were issued the armistice was signed. The savagery of Lindsay's designs may partly be attributed to his own ideas; but it also seems that savagery was considered a necessary element in the propaganda issued by countries such as Australia, which had no conscription.

2

3

1

4

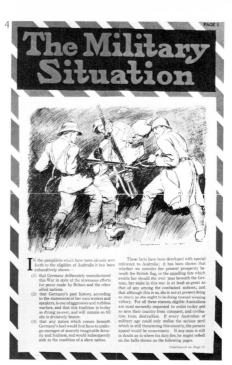

IWM Cat No: 0404

IWM Cat No: 3243

A German campaign

In Germany, where conscription was in force and recruiting posters were not needed, the energy of the government's propaganda organisation was channelled into campaigns to raise money by war loans. The Seventh War Loan campaign in 1917 used some particularly striking posters, such as Bernhard's *Das ist der Weg zum Frieden* (1) and Louis Oppenheim's *von Hindenburg* (see page 45). It also used much ephemeral material. Oppenheim contributed, besides his poster, a calendar (2) and a broadsheet, which shows in one of its images John Bull knocked out by 13·1 billion marks (3).

2

1

3

An American campaign

The American campaigns to raise war funds far surpassed even the German war loan campaigns. Admittedly the First Liberty Loan received little pictorial publicity and merely re-used the Uncle Sam figure familiar from recruiting posters (1); but for the Second Liberty Loan of 1917 more than five million posters were issued (one poster for every twenty people in the States). Adolph Treidler created for it the statue of Liberty logo of which a proof is shown here (2); it was used for every kind of visual propaganda from button-badges (3) to tube cards (4) and posters, such as Pennell's superb design (5) for the Fourth Liberty Loan of 1918. 500,000 copies of this poster were distributed and indeed a staggering total of ten million posters is said to have been used for this campaign.

I NEED YOU
if you can't fight – your money can
BUY A LIBERTY BOND NOW

I OWN A LIBERTY BOND

Owners of
LIBERTY LOAN BONDS
of the Second Liberty Loan of 1917
Wear this–
I OWN A LIBERTY BOND
BADGE OF HONOR

THAT LIBERTY SHALL NOT PERISH FROM THE EARTH
BUY LIBERTY BONDS
FOURTH LIBERTY LOAN

IWM Cat No: 0240

Hansi the propagandist

Jean Jacques Waltz (known as Hansi) produced a single-handed propaganda campaign. Using all kinds of visual propaganda he attacked the German occupation of Alsace and Lorraine, both by presenting an idealised picture of life there under French rule and by satirising the Germans. Thus he designed posters such as the one reproduced here (1), which shows a version of a new French Alsace Lorraine (the quotation from Victor Hugo says: 'This heaven is our blue sky, this field is our land. This Lorraine and this Alsace are ours!'); post-cards such as this one (2), which shows spring-time in Alsace; books such as *L'Alsace Heureuse* (Happy Alsace) whose frontispiece is reproduced (3) and broadsheets such as *El Dios Padre de su Majestad el Emperador Guillermo II* (Emperor William II's old God) which satirise the Germans, in this case by attacking an imaginary German God (4).

HANSI - Printemps en Alsace. (D'après l'estampe.)
Spring-time in Alsatia. (From the engraving.)

Typography

1914–18 posters display an interesting variety of typographic styles. In Britain the letterpress posters of the Parliamentary Recruiting Committee used a terrible jumble of wood and lead types (1). Note the chipping on some of the wood-printed letters in the poster illustrated here, and the shaky alignment and smudging which reflect the speed with which it was printed. It was one of the first war posters, produced in August 1914 in a run of 100,000. Very occasionally British artists designed their own lettering instead of letting the printers add it; for example Nevinson designed superb Futurist lettering for his *War* exhibition poster (2). In America this also happened; Howard Chandler Christy's hand-lettering has a frenzy that type could never emulate (3). In Germany and Austria many artists, such as Klinger and Bernhard, were also typographic designers. Indeed nearly all Bernhard's war posters were typographic, reviving the powerful impact of German print in previous ages (4).

IWM Cat No: 3289

IWM Cat No: 3508

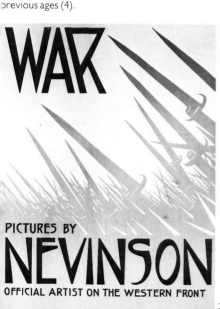

IWM Cat No: 0411

IWM Cat No: 0245

Animal symbols

1914–18 posters made considerable use of animal
symbolism. The cock on the poster shown here (1)
was, after Marianne (see page 62), the second
national symbol of France (the Latin word *gallus*
means both Gaul and cock). It was adopted during
the French Revolution when monarchist heraldic
symbols such as the fleur-de-lys were rejected.
The eagle, unlike the cock, was a heraldic bird,
symbol of Germany for many centuries (see page
30). On the French poster shown (2) it represents
an evil equal to tuberculosis and is symbolically
slain. The British Empire lion (3), one of the
national personifications of Great Britain, is
derived from the two supporters of the British
coat of arms, the Lion and the Unicorn. The
donkey in *Ich stimme Deutsch* (I vote German) was
not a national personification but a symbol of
ridicule for those Poles who voted for re-union
with Germany in 1921 (4). There was a poster
with the same donkey which declared *Ich stimme
Polnisch* (I vote Polish).

70

Plagiarism

Even during the war years posters were internationally exhibited: British recruiting posters were shown in Berlin in 1915, German commercial posters were exhibited in Grand Rapids, Michigan, in 1917, and posters of all the combatant nations were shown at Neuilly in 1917. They were also widely illustrated in magazines such as *The Poster* in America and *Das Plakat* in Germany. It is therefore hardly surprising that plagiarism was widespread. Sometimes the copy is better than the original. Klinger's Austrian War Loan poster of 1918 (1) is a far stronger image than its probable source, Willy Menz's German War Loan design of 1917 (2). In other cases however it is clear that there was one original design which was copied by several less able artists. Bernard Partridge's *Take up the Sword of Justice* (3) may not be a masterpiece, but the French and American versions (illustrated in *Das Plakat* which carried out several surveys of such plagiarism) are very poor imitations (4).

IWM Cat No: 3205

IWM Cat No: 0409

Display

War poster display varied considerably from country to country. British displays were, on the whole, appalling, reflecting the still low standards of commercial billboards throughout the country. The number of posters and their size was considered more important than their positioning. However, some commanding sites were used, for example this street corner at Liverpool (1). This was a practice continued in the 1939–45 war, when large buildings and monuments were covered with posters and banners. In strong contrast is the slickness of New Zealand poster display typified by the recruiting station which was constructed in Auckland in 1916–17 (2) and in America, as one might expect, vast posters were displayed on superb billboards in commanding positions. (3) shows four prominent St Louis businessmen who became bill-posters for the day to put up the 'paper' announcing the Second Liberty Loan of 1917.

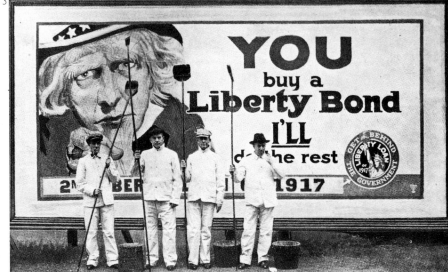